Praise for *In Transit*

"*In Transit* is a must-read for all audiences in pursuit of a sharper, more authentic understanding of the non-binary experience. Anderson confidently cuts through the noise of our cis-centered world, interweaving poignant accounts from queer history and outside LGBTQ+ perspectives. Above all, for those who feel displaced by dichotomies, this is a powerful, necessary reclamation of self and community."

—Eugene Lee Yang, writer, director,
actor, and digital producer

"*In Transit* provides a multifaceted look at what it means to be non-binary. Dianna Anderson recounts their own personal journey while simultaneously sharing the voices and stories of non-binary people who have traveled different pathways and come to understand themselves in diverse ways. Grounded in history and theory, yet always accessible, the book is an enlightening and enjoyable deep dive into this often overlooked and misunderstood identity."

—Julia Serano,
author of *Whipping Girl* and *Excluded*

"*In Transit* takes you through the history and theory behind the language that we use now to describe who we are, all while walking with Dianna Anderson in their journey to understand what that means for them. You'll find yourself captivated and educated by revealing tales throughout their life which may strike you as more familiar than you would expect regardless of where you are in the gender mosaic."

—Gavin Grimm,
trans activist and victor in the landmark lawsuit
Gavin Grimm v. Gloucester County School Board

"How can you explain who you are—to yourself and to others—when language itself is in transition? In this book Anderson paints a picture of the present moment while using a framework of travel and homecoming that will feel familiar to readers. I so appreciate that they don't shy away from the complexity of a discussion that is held both within and about gender-expansive communities. I know *In Transit* will encourage life-giving exploration."

—Austen Hartke,
author of *Transforming: The Bible and
the Lives of Transgender Christians*

"Anderson's *In Transit* is a much-needed work on non-binary identity. It is a great introductory text. I'm sure I'll be using chapters, if not the whole of the book, for my classes. A combination of personal history, relayed conversations, and research, *In Transit* provides an accessible, friendly, smart text for anyone seeking to understand non-binary identity."

—Helen Boyd,
author of *My Husband Betty:
Love, Sex, and Life with a Crossdresser*

IN TRANSIT

IN TRANSIT

Being Non-Binary in a
World of Dichotomies

Dianna E. Anderson

Broadleaf Books
Minneapolis

IN TRANSIT
Being Non-Binary in a World of Dichotomies

Cover design: Katie Lukes

Print ISBN: 978-1-5064-7924-8
eBook ISBN: 978-1-5064-7925-5

Printed in Canada

"I am the way I am. You are the way you are.
In a humane society the subject would be closed.
But this is not a humane society and so,
this is where my story begins."

—Diane Leslie Feinberg, *Journal of a Transsexual*, 1980

This book is dedicated to trans and gender-expansive,
gender-creative kids everywhere. Continue living your truth.
The world will catch up.

CONTENTS

Foreword   xi

Introduction   xiii

Glossary   xxi

    Chapter 1: Finding the Right Words   1

    Chapter 2: We Have Always Been Here   19

    Chapter 3: The Theory of Us   38

    Chapter 4: Finding a Home   57

    Chapter 5: Born and Becoming   71

    Chapter 6: Queer Possibilities, Queer Joy   89

    Chapter 7: Fat, Redistributed   106

    Chapter 8: The Expanse   124

    Chapter 9: Sisterhood, Not Cisterhood   141

    Chapter 10: Who Tells Your Story?   158

Acknowledgments   169

Notes   171

FOREWORD

Too often, our modern, try-hard media wants to acknowl-edge the existence of non-binary identities to seem hip and progressive and supportive. But the actual acknowl-edgment sometimes smacks of marketing. "Amazing," these stories suggest. "A new gender has been discovered. Now we have three!" It feels a little like when the addition of peanut butter M&Ms to the plain and peanut versions was treated as if a sacred mystery of the universe had been unlocked.

And, look, I know all the right things to say to explain how complicated and individual gender is, like, "Gender is a vast spectrum" and "Believe trans people when they say who they are." But those are marketing too, sort of. I believe they're true, but they're things we say to gloss over how weird and complicated and yucky the process of fig-uring yourself out can be. It's one thing to know gender is a vast spectrum. It's another to look at that vast spectrum, point to a spot, and say, "I think I belong there." And when you wind up there, you realize that spot is a vast spectrum too. It's spectrums all the way down.

Early in my own transition (hi, Emily, she/her), I had a recurring image pop into my brain in which I saw myself not as I was but as a suggestion of a person to be, a place-holder that only I knew how to make real. I used to refer to this in terms of sculpting and say I was "chiseling myself out of myself." Now I would probably soften that language because it sounds really painful to be chiseled, but the idea of slowly chipping away at the parts of yourself that don't make sense until you can find the person you are is one that, I hope, applies to everybody alive, regardless of their level of comfort with their gender assigned at birth.

The thing about this work is that it takes a lifetime. I've been living as a woman for years now, but I'm still learning things about my own womanhood that I find surprising, or frustrating, or validating. Instinctively, we all know that we're always evolving, but it's difficult to allow for both the pain and possibility of that evolution.

Trans people know this acutely, but even I have learned so much from my non-binary and gender-fluid friends about what it means to embrace self-discovery. That's why I'm so glad this book exists. My friend Dianna takes something complicated and in need of explanation (the slipperiness of gender) and somehow explains it via further complicating it. There are no easy answers. There are only vague destinations.

My favorite tarot card is the six of swords. In its most famous depiction, a figure huddled in a boat crosses a river, a wall of swords blocking them from seeing the other shore. It's a card about going somewhere without quite knowing where that somewhere is. You can probably see why this appeals to me, a trans woman, but I think we've all felt the uncertainty of not knowing how to get there from here.

We know there's a river. We don't know what's on the other side, but we have to cross anyway. Don't listen to anyone who tells you there's only the one boat. There are as many ways to cross it as there are people. I hope this book helps you find your way across, wherever you end up.

—*Emily VanDerWerff,* Critic at Large for *Vox*
September 21, 2021

INTRODUCTION

When I see birches bend to left and right
Across the lines of straight, darker trees,
I like to think some boy's been swinging them.

—Robert Frost, "Birches"

I grew up climbing trees. In my hometown of Sioux Falls, South Dakota, our house had multiple trees in the yard— huge old-growth maples and some middle-aged elm trees. The one that was easiest to get up into was also directly across from my bedroom. I'd climb up three stories and look across to realize I was level with the roof of the house. For a kid notoriously anxious about heights, climbing that tree felt safe: I was sure in my hands' ability to grip the branches, my legs' ability to brace themselves against lower branches, and the tree's sturdiness to support my back. The fact that children my age fell out of trees and hurt themselves seemed a strange fantasy to me—a thing that happened in books but not in real life, because surely other children felt the grip of the tree, tested the branches, and knew how high they could go before the tree branches would bend and snap under their weight.

I remember one Sunday when I was around eight. My parents had gotten me a new outfit for church, including shiny new dress shoes. We went to my aunt and uncle's house after the service, where a large old-growth oak tree wrapped around their deck, its thick and twisty trunk offering a tempting spot for a child to sit, above it all. Of course, I ignored the warnings about scratching my new shoes or tangling my new dress and clambered up to that seat, only to reluctantly be called down when my mother scolded me for damaging my new shoes, scuffing the shine off against the bark, leaving long scratches along the patent leather.

I don't remember seeing those shoes ever again, but I do remember that tree and that moment when I realized that being a proper girl meant not scratching up your shoes or climbing into a position where people could see up your dress. Over the next two decades, as I grew into an adult, I struggled with this tension between what I wanted to do and what I was allowed to do, with my body seeming to be an open season for commentary—aunts who worried that I wasn't eating enough, male doctors who warned me off sexual activity, youth pastors who instructed me to sit more properly and close my legs so I wasn't so open.

My girlhood was one of learning to close myself off, of listening to authorities instead of myself, of coming down out of the tree and realizing just how high I'd climbed. I don't remember my last time climbing that tree, though I suppose there must have been one. I must've one day swung down from the lowest branch, landing on the soft grass below for the last time, walking away from a childhood of calluses born of gripping the hard bark of the tree, scrapes along my back from bracing myself against its trunk as I moved from branch to branch on my way up.

At some point, we put away those things that made us feel free and alive as children. I don't think we do so consciously. As we learn more in school, learn to explore other worlds through the wonder of books, develop friendships that rely more on conversation than on play, we drift away from the temptation of climbing that tree and into the roles we've built for each other—we become friends, lovers, wives, husbands, adults. We come into our own and realize who we are and who we want to become. And we realize the ways in which we are and always were different from the norm, whether that means coming into our own gender or sexuality, or finally getting that diagnosis for an atypical presentation of attention deficit hyperactivity disorder (ADHD), or simply understanding and working through our trauma. We learn to use community to develop who we are, working with others as sounding boards to discover our own truths.

I'm in my thirties now. I've spent the last decade unpacking most of the lessons I learned about the roles of men and women in the world. I've come out to myself and the world as a lesbian. And now, the more and more I think about what it means to be my very self, the more and more the label of "woman" feels incorrect, a label imposed by forces outside of me. I get ads on social media for transgender clothing lines designed with special pockets for trans men to hold their modeled prosthetic penises, ads for articles about how to bind safely. I've been called "sir" multiple times throughout my life, though as I've gained weight and my breasts became more prominent, that has faded away—even as my hair has gotten shorter and shorter. I find myself looking back at that time when my best friends were guys, when we spent our days doing boyish things, climbing up trees and staring back through the window into my bedroom with its bright pink carpet and stuffed animals. I knew that girl from back then never quite sat right in her gender, either, even though she was fine and happy with who she was.

Am I non-binary? A voice began to whisper the question in 2018, though I ignored it for a long time. Coming out as a different gender would surely be harder than it was to come out as a lesbian. "I'm gay" was a statement I didn't have to explain. "I'm non-binary" would be. I'd have to change my titles, start going by "Entle" instead of "Aunt," teach new bosses about "Mx.," and take on the task of explaining who I am to each new person. Am I ready for that emotional load? Am I *trans*?

I started reading. I started researching. I went back to my women's studies texts from five years before, when I completed my master's in the subject. I read up on queer theory from back in the 1990s and the 2000s and learned about all the divisions and debates about the place of transgender, gender-fluid, and gender-nonconforming people within the queer community. But I couldn't find what I needed: a book that walked me through what it's like, inside, when you realize that your gender is different from the one you were assigned at birth. Trans memoirs were too linear for me. I didn't see myself reflected in the common stories told about trans people—the person assigned male at birth who always knew they were a girl and, like a butterfly, metamorphosed into a beautiful feminine woman. As much as I love Laverne Cox, her journey did not necessarily speak to mine as a frumpy fat person from the Midwest who was not fab or fierce.

I also found a debate about the role non-binary people play in the queer community and not a lot of dedicated work to teasing out how that looks in real life. In what ways does the gender-nonconforming community overlap with the transgender one? Are we the same? Or are we separate entities? Here, I found a raging debate but no real answers. I needed a book for me that laid out the theory, the experience, the life, the desires, the journey.

So I decided to write that book, for all the tree-climbing girls who grew up to question their girlhood, for all the people who never felt they fit, and for all the people for whom looking down at their bodies causes physical pain. Maybe we can finally synthesize all the different arguments happening within the community and develop a lexicon that is accurate, an argument that resonates, and a conclusion that doesn't erase experiences.

My hope is that you will take from this book an exploration of what it means to be non-binary, what it means to be trans, and learn to find the vocabulary for yourself. This is your journey as much as it is mine, so you deserve to learn about how we got this language to begin with, how the theory developed to explain existing lived experiences in our community. And I want you to come along with me to learn about how non-binary people have always been here, how we have existed, hidden between the cisnormative pages of history books, living our lives in ways that challenge historians to this day to explain.

In writing this book, I seek to explore and explain the linguistic and social problems we encounter when we try to lump all parts of a broad, diverse community under the same umbrella. When we say that anyone who deviates from their gender assigned at birth is trans, we are making a specific declarative statement that will necessarily be inadequate to explain all experiences. I seek here to separate out non-binary from the trans community and provide a definition that works for those of us who don't necessarily experience dysphoria or a medical diagnosable condition. In doing this, I work to tease out the different models we have for talking about gender and develop a new one that fits for those of us who are "non." Where do we fit? Can I be a non-binary lesbian? Can such a category exist? I hope to answer those questions and more here in this book.

This book is for people who have some familiarity with gender theory, and it contains refreshers for those who may have set Butler and de Beauvoir down a long time ago. It delves into the work of 1990s queer theory as an intersecting locus of activism and academia, working through the different ways trans people have described themselves and how people who didn't fit into the binary described themselves ("genderfuck" is a favorite term of mine from that era). By grounding ourselves in this understanding, we will be able to understand the current moment, where online communities have come to play a much larger role in developing and understanding gender within and without community. It looks forward to a world where being who we are, whatever that looks like, isn't met with tension and long-winded explanations but rather acceptance and love.

In 1991, trans theorist Sandy Stone argued in a groundbreaking paper that the reason anti-trans discourses like Janice Raymond's *The Transsexual Empire* took such hold was because much of the broad public understanding of transsexuality resulted in a flattening of the subjectivity of trans experiences.[1] At the time of her writing, transsexuality was narrated largely as a person is "born in the wrong body," and medical steps are needed to "correct" the problem. Once the person's transition is medically complete, they are then encouraged to develop a false history in which they have always been the gender they are presenting as. This narrative, pushed upon the trans community by medical and psychological gatekeepers (which I will explore in part one of this book), results in trans narratives being erased entirely from the ongoing discourse. This cedes the floor to our critics and allows them to shape the public narrative about our lives.

Stone proposes an alternate route: that trans people take back their own subjectivity, that they refuse to allow their stories to be flattened, that they refuse to "pass" into obscurity. For many, this is an impossible burden to ask—it is the upending of lives, the confrontation of painful pasts, the embrace of dissonance long put away.

But Stone was writing in a time when "genderqueer" was a nascent political and social identity. In the thirty years since, non-binary has emerged as a new discourse on gender, a new vision for how we perform and understand the self through the lens of gender. This new category deserves its own discourse, born out of the work of the transsexual movement, absorbed into the idea of transgender, and now, finally, emerging as its own thing. After all, the goal of non-binary identity is *never* to "pass" as a singular gender but rather, by our very existence, challenge and deconstruct the ways assumptions and presuppositions about gender altogether. This is our coming out, our embrace of the discourse, our stories told by us, our way of approaching and understanding gender as a genre and a discourse.

—

To help us along, I've also included a glossary of terms as they are used in this work to ensure that we are starting from the same page. Some terms I use may strike readers as out of date or unusual for the progressive framework, so I have included explanations as to why I choose specific terms like "transgenderism" as acknowledgment of the historical role they have played in queer theory. As our goal here is to come to a workable definition of a term in wide use, defining the terms surrounding the term in question is vital to the project at hand. Note that "non-binary" and "transgender" are not defined here as that is the objective of this book.

GLOSSARY

AMAB/AFAB (Assigned Male at Birth/Assigned Female at Birth). The assignment given by a doctor based upon observation of external gentalia at birth.

Binder. A chest compression garment worn by non-binary and trans masc-identified AFAB people to flatten their breasts and give the illusion of maleness.

Bottom Surgery. Either a phalloplasty, which involves adding a penis by taking skin from elsewhere in the body and rerouting the urethra, or a vaginoplasty, wherein the penis is inverted to create a vaginal canal.

Cisgender. A person for whom the gender assigned at birth and the gender they feel they are match up.

Clocking/Reading. Being read or clocked means someone has figured out that you are trans without you telling them. It is usually used to mean that you did not pass as cisgender in a given situation.

Deep Stealth. A trans person who, after corrective surgeries, chooses not to disclose their trans status and instead fully assimilates into their gender.

Detransition/Detrans/Desist. These terms refer to a person who at one point identified as trans but has since returned to identifying as their assigned sex at birth.

Ethnography. A scientific approach to studying a people group that involves gathering information about how people within a people group describe themselves and then using those terms as descriptive understandings of how the people in that group interact and understand social situations.

Gender. An identity you have in your head of who you are, informed by social categories that change depending on cultural artifacts and signals (e.g., a woman in Japan may engage in ceremonial kimono wearing as an expression of their gender within that society, while a woman in the United States tends toward wearing makeup and heels to signify and perform their gender).

Gender Dysphoria. A painful experience where the gender one is in their mind does not match with their physical body, often causing psychic and physiological distress.

Gender Euphoria. The opposite of dysphoria, it is the feeling of pleasure/happiness one experiences upon having their gender performance recognized as the gender they were aiming for.

Intersex. A person whose gender at birth is not assigned to either binary option due to a condition where their genitals present ambiguously and/or contain elements of the binary sexual options.

Passing. When a trans person is read as their actual gender versus the one assigned at birth.

Sex. The physical representation of one's assigned gender, appearing biologically in the genitals and in secondary sex characteristics such as breasts or facial hair.

Sexuality. An identity formed based on who you are or are not attracted to. Variations include but are not limited to gay, straight, lesbian, bisexual, pansexual, and asexual.

T/E/HRT. These initials are shorthand for synthetic testosterone or estrogen, collectively known as hormone replacement therapy. These hormones are used in medical transition to make a person's body more like that of their gender identity in either masculinizing or feminizing ways.

The Binary. The two different options for gender according to a heteronormative and cisnormative power structure: man or woman. These options sit on the binary ends of a spectrum of gender.

Top Surgery. A surgery removing or adding breast tissue to effect either a flat chest or creating breasts.

Transgenderism/Transgenderist. An older term from the 1970s/'80s used to discuss people who do not necessarily conform to either gender and act as an advocate for demolishing or deconstructing what a gender role is.

Transsexual or Transexual. An older term (mid-twentieth century up to around 2000) for binary trans individuals who saw themselves as "born in the wrong body" and sought medical intervention to correct that issue and obtain a body that reflects their vision of their gender.

1

FINDING THE RIGHT WORDS

O Earth, that hast no voice, confide to me a voice!
O harvest of my lands! O boundless summer growths!
O lavish, brown, parturient earth! O infinite, teeming womb!
A verse to seek, to see, to narrate thee.

—Walt Whitman, *Leaves of Grass*

Before I was born, my parents had two boys. They expected—unscientifically, but as every parent does—that their third would be no different. Mom was prepared to remain a minority in the house no matter what, and my brothers were ready for a little brother they could play with.

To everyone's surprise, I was pulled out of my mother via C-section, a screaming, crying, seven-pound baby girl. My dad was so thrilled he immediately drove to the local department store and bought two extremely frilly baby dresses for me. I cannot emphasize just how frilly and lacy these dresses were. In my baby pictures, I am a head sticking out of a sea of white lace. It was the '80s.

And thus my life began, pulled from my mother only to be shoved into a pile of frills.

Despite my mother's best efforts, I was not a child who embraced the more delicate and frilly aspects of life. I fell out of the car playing with my brothers and got a concussion at five. Over the next few years, I slammed my head into a door, requiring stitches, and then slammed my head into the bathroom counter, requiring yet another set of stitches. My favorite color was blue, despite clear attempts to steer me toward pink. I refused to let my parents brush my long, wavy hair, necessitating a bowl cut from Grandma Darlene—who at least was a professional hairdresser and kept the short haircut from being a complete disaster. I found myself bonding most easily with the boys at school, playing in the dirt, being king of the mountain, and handling the unfortunate garter snake that wandered into the playground, while the girls played house, built snowmen, and screamed when we came at them with the snake.

When I learned what the word "tomboy" meant, I declared that was me.

I grew up already knowing that "being a girl" was something you shaped and formed for yourself. My parents didn't try to force me into any one role—they let me be as wild and playful as I wanted to be. Little bits of gender roles crept in with moments like my brother being taught how to mow the lawn while my job was to dust the furniture. But looking back, I'm not so sure that was a gender thing so much as a "Dianna is so clumsy she'll probably lose a limb" thing (as mentioned, by the time I was eight, I'd already ended up in urgent care twice for stitches).

Having such freedom meant that when I arrived at graduate school in my early twenties, I was primed to take on feminist studies, though I didn't admit it at the time. In college, I'd embraced a far more traditional role for myself, delving deeply into evangelical Christian culture and accepting but chafing at the idea that because I was a woman, my job was forever meant as a support role to the men in my life. Because evangelical culture told me marriage was the ultimate expression of G-d's love, I longed to be married. Once, I frustratedly turned to a male friend of mine and asked him what was wrong with me—why don't guys show any interest or ask me out?

"You're intimidating," came the response. "You're super smart and outmatch a lot of us."

So there was another tick on the list of "things a Good Christian Woman shouldn't be": smart. It was this moment when I think a part of me broke. I was the daughter of two teachers, brought up in a home where I learned to read and write before I even hit kindergarten. I was an A student, devoured books, and wrote essays for fun. For me, a good night in college wasn't staying up until 3:00 a.m. talking about boys—it was staying up until three talking about predestination and child baptism. I used words like "salvific" in everyday conversation.

And apparently intimidated men.

This criticism hit me in the place that hurt the most. I could take whatever comments people felt like hurling about my awkward gangly frame, about my choice of haircut—by then, back to a pixie cut—or my inability to do makeup. I could take criticisms about me being annoying, even. By then I'd accepted that some personalities and mine just don't get along.

But to say that men found me intimidating because I was smart hit a new low, right at the center of my own construction of selfhood. I was being pressured to diminish a fundamental part of myself for the sake of finding a person to love me, and I could not bring myself to do it. At that point, a baby feminist was born. I discovered a boundary within myself that balked at the idea that I should give up parts of who I am simply because men found them scary.

A year later, I was in a graduate literary theory class at Baylor University, looking at the course assignments and staring at my name next to the words "Queer Theory." Being a Christian at a "distinctly Baptist" university, I was a little surprised that we were covering queer theory at all. But more than that, I wanted to take on the theory my friend had been assigned: feminist theory. By then, I'd begun to call myself a feminist and was developing an understanding of the world under this new lens. But thanks to the ordering of the alphabet, I would have to present a conference paper on queer theory and essentially teach the concept to the rest of my class.

I wasn't ready for what happened to me once I did the work.

I chose to write on and analyze the movie *Mulan* (then only existing in animated form). I wrote about how the story plays with gender presentation, accepting that everything is largely a performance, and Mulan's ability is not diminished by coming into her girlhood as a fully realized human. She is both made into a man and becomes a girl worth fighting for. The central song, "I'll Make a Man Out of You," is also a deeply trans turning point: Mulan, as Ping, learns to imitate and perform manhood as well as, if not better than, the cisgender men around her.

My world sprang open with this one study. Gender as a socially constructed performance would inform everything I did over the next decade: coming out, cutting off all my hair, choosing to eschew or adopt femininity as I saw fit, embracing my own queerness.

This eye-opening experience is why I always start out with theory. Theory gave me the language to understand myself, define my space within the world, and consider the ways in which we think about the self and the other, in all the queerest ways.

Let's start with the feminists. The primary text with which to engage when talking about defining gender is French philosopher Simone de Beauvoir's epic tome in multiple parts: *The Second Sex*. A member of France's philosopher class that arose in the early nineteenth century, de Beauvoir was steeped in the emerging thought of French existentialism—the questions of what man is, what man does, and who man grows to be. A longtime partner of philosopher Jean-Paul Sartre, both in sparring debate over philosophy and in matters of the heart, de Beauvoir couldn't help but notice that the philosophy world was something of a boys' club.

And, she noticed, this boys' club mentality left gaps in their knowledge, especially as they assumed "man" to be a stand-in for the everyday human. A "man" could be assumed to be the default across the board in philosophy, while women constantly stood as Other. She takes the argument in two parts, first examining the station of woman as it is created through the biological reality of pregnancy and labor. A woman's reproductive utility and role as the bearer of the human species, she contends, is part and parcel of why men see "woman" as the Other. Men evince disgust at the everyday reality of women, contending that menstruating women are "unclean." Because of this Othering and disgust, men have created myths about women to explain their subjugation as deserved, a necessary protection of their femininity, casting men as the heroes and women as the unknowable, uncharted territory that must be conquered.

Jumping off from the point of biological understandings, de Beauvoir devotes the latter volume of *The Second*

Sex to exploring what makes a woman a woman. In philosophical terms, she is examining female ontology—or beingness—and creating a knowledge base, or epistemics, around it. You may well be familiar with her most famous phrase: "One is not born, but rather becomes, a woman."[1] She opens the second volume with this declaration, starting from how womanhood is viewed and shaped throughout childhood, adolescence, and adulthood.

Here we are introduced to the idea that a gender is not inherent at birth but rather made through the collective action of response to outward and inward stimuli. De Beauvoir essentially proposes that a woman's life lived in service of a man's ideal—becoming a wife, a mother, or a housekeeper and forever being tasked with menial chores—is what informs and gives voice to this idea of "womanhood" as a thing outside the person itself. We are socially conditioned in what makes us "woman," from the moment our parents put us in frilly lace dresses to our first sexual encounters with men who take for themselves without thought for our pleasure.

This unfettering of "womanhood"—and, subsequently, "manhood"—from an innate, biological physiology was the start of gender theory as we know it. It was this unlinking that spawned a thousand articles and books about what it means to be a woman and how we come to those conclusions. Much of philosophical thought, to this point, imagined one's status as a man or a woman as a given—that how you are perceived meant you carried with you innate characteristics of that identity. Women were subservient because it was a biological reality that they were.

But de Beauvoir broke all of that apart, proposing instead that women are forced into subservience because of the habitual way men are taught to view them. It is the gaze of men upon women that creates the (mis)conception of womanhood as a specific thing in itself rather than a set of cultural cues that are conditioned into us from birth.

For me, this was a revelation. I'd always vaguely known stuff about how gender is perceived and built, but here was a woman arguing it in black and white: that what we know of womanhood and manhood is the result of culturally conditioned thought and therefore bound by the same.

Around the same time I was reading de Beauvoir for literary theory, I was also being introduced to another Simone—French philosopher Simone Weil. A Christian who rejected Judaism and the Old Testament,[2] Weil was a modern Christian mystic philosopher. Weil's theory of creation stemmed from the idea of absence: G-d must withdraw from the world in order to create. G-d, as all perfect, cannot create that which is imperfect, so for humanity to be free, G-d withdrew from the world and deliberately limited G-dself so that creation could occur.[3] In working to embody G-d in the world, then, it is a Christian's duty to likewise empty themselves and love their neighbor so fully that the self disappears. Weil was also deeply entranced by the idea that the self is made, not innate, and that our sense of "I" only comes from circumstances of birth. People could make choices to change themselves, but the influence of those choices was a matter of circumstance.

For instance, I, a white person born to white parents in South Dakota, am only who I am because of the circumstances of my birth. There is no ethereal Dianna toward which I may grasp; rather, that "I," which has been formed and developed by my circumstances, is the only "I" to which I have access.

It was in seeing this idea of the "I" as grounded in conditioning, circumstances, and lived experience that meant the most to me. Reading all these philosophers at the same time was a pure coincidence of my class schedule, but the impact it had was not. My conception of what it meant to be me was exploding and reforming. By the time I landed at Judith Butler,[4] it felt like I was arriving at home base. Here was this new understanding that spoke to how I was beginning to see the world.

Butler is a tough nut to crack for people who are unaccustomed to academic speak—much of Butler's formal language reads as obtuse and impenetrable, full of allusions to previous works. It's clear that the reader would be familiar enough with the ongoing conversation that speaking to the layperson was not on Butler's mind. And I believe you readers are smart enough to grasp their meaning but may not have the context from which to do so.

Butler's most famous book (and rightly so) is 1990's *Gender Trouble*. In it, they offer the final puzzle pieces of an argument about gender, pulling on what was already by then a large cadre of feminist philosophers, including Wittig, Lévi-Strauss (not the jeans company), Irigaray, hooks, and French postmodernists Derrida, Foucault, and Lacan. Speaking from their position as a lesbian theoretician, Butler positions de Beauvoir's ideas of womanhood in conversation with homosexuality, seeking to elucidate how gender is constructed alongside assumed heterosexuality. But to go there, we need to step back into the discussion of language itself, which is the primary discussion being had by Butler and which will be undertaken throughout the rest of this book.

Something happened in the twentieth century where numerous philosophers began to undertake the problems of how we think about and describe reality. Starting largely with Ludwig Wittgenstein, continental philosophy began to turn inward, to look at the very words we use to describe the world and to communicate. Wittgenstein was an Austrian philosopher who studied under Bertrand Russell at Cambridge and later held his own professorship there. He was continually plagued by the question of how a person conveys meaning: language is itself defined by its usage. In asking what a word means, then, a person—a speaker—must use the word, rendering circular the question of asking for meaning.

What he proposes is a short thought exercise: think in your head for the moment and define the word "game."

Then think about this: how can the word "game" both mean children playing tag in the park and the men sitting still at a table puzzling over chess?[5]

This tension is the central one that Wittgenstein explores: that language we have becomes itself as we use it. We must, as humans, grapple with the meaning of words as we use them, determining resemblances between ideas as represented by words, and, finally, decide whether to abide by the rules as constructed by language or reject them—decisions we make each time we speak.

Wittgenstein also proposed that language is fundamentally a communal act, which is perhaps his most important argument. Because language develops its meaning within its use, it is impossible to have a private language, or one that is only relevant to the individual, because such language would be impossible to understand by any other human. The lack of communal meaning applied to a language renders the language inert and unusable—and an unusable language is no language at all. It is this fundamental aspect of communal understanding from which all of life must flow.[6]

To use a modern example, money is fake. There is no intrinsic or inherent value in a dollar bill. I can set it on fire, and nothing significant will happen besides some funny-colored smoke. But we, collectively, as a community, have agreed to give it value by believing in money and a market as a concept. We have collectively developed and agreed to a shared delusion that tiny metal coins and slips of paper—or, in contemporary settings, series of zeroes and ones on an electronic record—constitute "currency," and with this currency we can "purchase" the necessary items for survival.

It's all bullshit, but we give it meaning.

There is, of course, a lot more to Wittgenstein. But what Wittgenstein began was a philosophical rabbit hole that led to the broad opening of critical theory as it stands today. Following Wittgenstein, and pulling in from new psychoanalytic sciences and a developing philosophy of the mind, French postmodern theorists like the two Jacques—Derrida and Lacan—and their contemporary Jean Baudrillard worked on variations of a theme, deconstructing and reforming language as humans who are creating that language at the same time.

Derrida, the father of deconstructionism, attempts to find a relationship between meaning and form. Rejecting the idea of a Platonic ideal—that is, rejecting that there is one universal, let's say, tree out there from which all other trees are merely representations—Derrida proposes that meaning derives from the appearance of a meaning. Most importantly, Derrida proposed that terms such as "truth" and "justice" are far too complex and carry so much baggage that their meanings become obscured and irrevocably complicated.[7] Your evangelical father might call this the beginnings of moral relativism, but it's a bit more complicated than that. Because we build meaning both individually and culturally after we have deconstructed "traditional" meanings—that is, worked to determine those meanings within our current cultural context, taking cues from what we mean *now*—we can then proceed in something of a reconstruction.

Baudrillard builds on Derrida's points about meaning and proposes that, in the age of mass production, we have largely lost hold of true meaning and therefore rely on the simulation of a thing for meaning. The simulation of the thing then becomes the thing in itself.[8] The *Matrix* movies function as a good shorthand for Baudrillard here: Neo lives in what he believes to be reality until he is shown that the reality he is in is merely a simulation of what used to be real, and it is what Baudrillard would term "hyperreal."[9] He proposed in the 1980s that we are currently in the era of simulation and not yet at hyperreal but on our way there. Essentially, because of mass production, there was a loss of genuinely unique things in the world, replaced by a mere simulation of the real, with the real having disappeared, no longer reachable. Your IKEA sofa is not a unique object in itself, but a replica of an original design, repeated over and over until its resemblance to the original is lost: copies of copies of copies. To apply Baudrillard to gender, then, is to say that gender exists as a simulation, as a copy of a thing that no longer exists as itself (a copy of the material property of sex, as it were).

This brings us back to Butler. Taking into account the idea that language really only has the meanings that we bestow upon it as its creators and users, Butler proposes that gender functions like language in that it only really has the ability to imitate and represent, not convey meaning in itself. Butler writes that the "tacit constraints that produce culturally intelligible 'sex' ought to be understood as generative political structures rather than naturalized foundations."[10] Essentially, because we only have our cultural understanding and our cultural boundaries from which to talk about "male" and "female," we will never be describing the thing itself but rather everything we know around the thing. It is continually produced as a thing that exists in time and in specific historical cultural moments and has been consistently expanded over time.

Butler points back to Wittgenstein's discourse on rule following when stating that "such appearances are rule-generated identities, ones which rely on the consistent and repeated invocation of rules that condition and restrict culturally intelligible practices of identity. Indeed, to understand identity as a practice and as a signifying practice, is to understand culturally intelligible subjects as the resulting effects of a rule-bound discourse that inserts itself in the pervasive and mundane signifying acts of linguistic life."[11]

We have rules about how we use language around gender. We are brought up being conditioned into these rules and learn how to perform to meet the strictures of those rules by repeated habit of practice. Identity—particularly gender—is not sprung whole cloth out of some mystical, ethereal plane but is instead the continued, habitual practice of following the rules of our society set up for genders. Women are women because they consistently practice their gender in ways that have been largely culturally agreed upon as "womanhood."

Butler uses the prevalence of drag queens as an example of the ways in which "womanhood" is stretched and rules-tested by otherwise cisgender men. Butler says that drag, as quite literal performance in gay male spaces, "reveals the imitative structure of gender itself. . . . In the place of the law of heterosexual coherence, we see sex and gender denaturalized by means of a performance which avows their distinctness and dramatizes the cultural mechanism of their fabricated unity."[12] Because "womanhood" is so easily taken as performance (and manhood likewise, with drag kings), the very existence of such persons as entertainers is a big middle finger to the rules about gender.

The thing about rules is that they can be broken. We can make visible the cultural apparatus that inscribes meaning upon the body and make it known. We can intervene in the performance and consciously make movements toward changing it. In those everyday mundane signifying acts, we can subvert and determine gender differently. Gender is not tied to the body, except and only insofar as the body is a place upon which we place meaning.

Gender, therefore, is what we make it. We repeat performances like a theater constantly playing a matinee with subtle changes with every showing—that is, if we accept the premises of postmodern philosophy, which must be grappled with in order to have any coherent conversation about gender.

Many critics of this philosophical foundation have argued that postmodern philosophy by the likes of Derrida and Butler goes too far in presuming that the deconstruction of language and identity are possible. Such philosophy, critics say, deconstructs the "old religions" of science, logic, and reason, arguing that because we create meaning, we cannot possibly arrive at reason as a common ground between sides of an argument, and there is no objective Truth (with a capital T).

This, however, is the fundamental undertaking of this book—how do we define and discuss gender apart from and connected to the binary? Who is trans? Who is nonbinary? Who are we as a community?

Trans theorist Susan Stryker poignantly writes that transgender identity itself forces a reckoning with the language we have to talk about ourselves: we must reexamine what the very categories of "man" and "woman" mean. That reckoning can create anger: "The rage itself is generated by the subject's situation in a field governed by the unstable but indissoluble relationship between language and materiality that simultaneously eludes definitive representation and demands its own perpetual rearticulation in symbolic terms."[13] We use language to create materiality—we understand gender through a common language, and trans identities disrupt that previously stable regulatory system. Trans people, Stryker argues, do not have a choice in upending the regulatory systems of gender; they are "compelled to enter a 'domain of objected bodies, a field of deformation' that in its unlivability encompasses and constitutes the realm of legitimate subjectivity."[14]

Because trans people are forced at once to deform themselves from "the natural order," their very existence calls attention to the fragility of that order itself. Stryker notes that many people do not acquiesce easily to being termed "creature" because it forces them away from the illusion that they are the makers and lords of creation.[15] Instead, we are subject to "a gendering violence [that is] the founding condition of human subjectivity."[16] Think back to the 1990s and the central *Saturday Night Live* character "It's Pat!" The entire conceit of the sketch is that no one can accurately tell what gender Pat is because their presentation, ways of speaking, and general presence resist categorization. So people around Pat ask them questions that should give clues to the person's gender, to which Pat persists in answering in specific non-gendered ways. The fact that Pat resists categorization is played for laughs, but in the real world, the inability to categorize often creates an excuse for gendered violence—because a person flouts the categories and forces people to reckon with their own presumptions of categories, those not ready for that conversation often react with rage and violence.

For cisgender people, this "gendering violence" is only highlighted in more abstract ways. They are aware of the roles society asks everyone to play and are fine bending the rules around themselves as cis people. But transgender bodies, Stryker proposes, offer such an upending that their very existence calls into question the natural order: "To encounter the transsexual body, to apprehend a transgendered consciousness articulating itself, is to risk a revelation of the constructedness of the natural order."[17]

Butler revisited their work in *Gender Trouble* over and over in the three decades since it was first published in 1990 and remarked in a 2021 interview with British writer Owen Jones that they had spent a lot of time encountering and incorporating trans critiques in their work. As a result, they now offer a couple of caveats about the idea of gender as performance or social construction. First is that the assertion that gender is performance does *not* mean that gender is somehow "chosen." It's "deep-seated and historically formed and our struggle to make something new is one that takes place in that historical situation."[18] Change happens over time, bit by bit, as we repeat performances and find what works, what doesn't, and what feels correct for ourselves.

Their second caveat is that saying gender is constructed through social and historical performance does not mean that gender is fake or false. Gender is a social, historical, and political reality that comes into play in our individual everyday lives in very material ways. Saying that gender is the product of repeated performances means that we are operating within social and historical categories that give meaning to specific ideas about those performances and that the goal of feminism should be to change how those material realities are perceived.

Butler is also very sensitive to the ways in which language shapes and creates our world. "Trans" feels to us, here in the early 2020s, like it has been around for a long time, but it's really only in my short millennial lifetime that "transgender" has become a term at all. Butler points out, again in the Jones interview, that such linguistic shifts raise the question, Are trans people who existed before we had the term "trans" actually trans, or are they some other thing? The question of how language creates and instills meaning is a vitally important one as we move forward in determining what we want the queer community to look like.

—

I was in elementary school the first time I heard the word "faggot." One of my classmates had it as a favorite word—I don't know where he learned it, but I suspect it was at home. I didn't know what it meant, aside from it being "bad." This was the 1990s, a time when euphemisms raged on the playground. We fifth graders made jokes about "doing it," even though we weren't quite sure what "it" even was. It was a time in my life when all my friends were guys, and I thought being a girl meant I should chase boys on the playground. I heard the kids call each other "fag" and used it all of once, only to be scolded by a teacher who must've been horrified at the casual nature of an absolutely terrible insult, not "a bundle of sticks" like kids said when they were asked if they know what it means.

I learned the word around the time Matthew Shepard and Brandon Teena were murdered. I didn't know yet what a faggot was—or even that I was one. For our elementary-school conversations, it was an "adult" term we knew to throw around at each other if we really wanted to stick it to someone. These encounters, I recognize now, shaped my perception of the term. I was steeped in homophobia and transphobia, and our cultural cues about what was correct for one's performed gender were shaped and calculated by the ongoing presence of that homophobia. Because of the ways in which my language was restricted and denied to me as a young person, I, like many other millennials, am only just now realizing who I am.

Our first step toward comprehending the role that non-binary identities play in our cultural framework is developing a mutual understanding of an ultimately shaky and easily misunderstood idea. We cannot communicate if we do not agree to speak the same language, and we must pull apart what we mean by "man" and "woman"—or, as is the project of this work, "trans" and "non-binary"—before we can ever hope to move forward in justice. We must confront the homophobia and transphobia inherent in how we talk about our own genders.

It took me an extremely long time to come around to the idea that I might be non-binary largely because I was terrified of what it would mean to transition. I wanted to be OK just staying in my little closet, closed off from the rest of the world, pretending that "she" and "her" were OK and accurate. I had a literal phobia around the idea that I might need to avail myself of hormones, surgery, and special clothing. I worried about explaining myself to others, having to do the work of educating them on what "non-binary" actually means. And I recognized that with many, the problem, by and large, was that we lacked mainstream cultural understanding of gender variance.

It is not that truth does not exist; it is that truth is hard to develop a communal definition of.

To explore these ideas, we need to understand that both our visions of ourselves and how we move within space and time are shaped by our past and our ideas of what gender is and what it can become. As a person assigned female at birth, my gender journey will look different from someone designated male at birth, and each of these experiences contributes to the whole of a diverse community. We are creating our own theory of our lives as we move forward, knowing that the tension of exchange, debate, and critique are all vital to the development of a stable home base wherein we know who we are and where we came from. How we comport ourselves will look different from everyone else around us, and that's OK. We are becoming who we are with each new movement and each new idea.

2

WE HAVE ALWAYS BEEN HERE

Soon the day will come when science will win a victory over error, justice a victory over injustice, and human love a victory over human hatred and ignorance.

—Dr. Magnus Hirschfeld at the 1919 premier of
Different from the Others, the first-known film
featuring a love story between gay men

At my undergraduate college, where I was studying theology, Church History was a required course for the major. The class was taught by Dr. B, a serious man who is one of the nation's foremost scholars on the theologian Karl Barth. Dr. B had been a basketball player in college, but his sporty days appeared to have been left behind long ago, replaced by a balding hairline, pressed button-up shirts, and Eddie Bauer khaki pants and loafers. He wrote out his lectures longhand and had no patience for distraction or questions that weren't immediately relevant to the subject. He was intimidating but not unreachable. At one point, one of our theology major cohort heard a rumor that he is afraid of ketchup, which we decided to test out when he joined us in the cafeteria for lunch. Each of us had grabbed a small cup of ketchup for our fries, and while he was in line, we placed the cups surrounding his spot at the table, creating a small half-oval around where his tray would go. When he returned carrying his tray of food, he saw what we had done and stood obstinately behind his chair, refusing to sit down until we had moved the offending condiment.

Despite the friendship we had, Dr. B's Church History course was not easy. Taking advice from the seniors who had already been through the ringer with the course, we formed study groups with flash cards to remember dates, names, councils, and sermons from a two-thousand-year history of the Christian church. We visited a Greek Orthodox church (the only one in our small city in South Dakota) to learn about their traditions and specifically their theology around the concept of sin. When we got to Martin Luther's 95 Theses and the Protestant Reformation, one of our fellow students taped a set of twenty-five theses to Dr. Bender's office door, offering such complaints as "Professors should allow a longer grace period for late papers." Dr. Bender's only comment on that was "You couldn't think of ninety-five?"

I eventually made it through that class but not after having an embarrassing brain fart trying to remember the name of the leader of the Visigoths who sacked Rome in the year 410 (Alaric is the answer; I put Frank). And sure enough, this piece of history is literally the only fact from the class that I remember going on fifteen years later. I know the basic points of history, but what I mainly remember is that we spent a lot of time talking about the actions of white cisgender men, many of whom were obsessed with the machinations of the institutional church, and many others (like the popes we studied) were deeply invested in the preservation of the institution. As a person who, at the time, identified as a woman and wanted to go into ministry in some capacity, I remember feeling disheartened as colorful card after card flashed by in our study sessions with male name after male name. Thomas Aquinas. Martin Luther. John Calvin. St. Augustine of Hippo. Ulrich Zwingli. The long march of patriarchs laid out before us in flash cards, on our test answer sheets, and in the history of our church. I felt my status as a marginalized person in those moments, though I didn't yet have the words for it. What I knew and felt in my bones was that history has largely been the story of men—their wars, their marriages, their treaties, their ideas, and their bodies. I couldn't articulate it then, but I sensed that we were being given a skewed version of history, one that, yes, gave us dates and historical events but one that also flattened out the church into a story of men persevering and women just kind of along for the ride.

But, of course, real life and real history are far more complicated. History is itself far more complex than a memorized set of facts as though advances happened in a linear fashion. Even as I'd been taught that history consisted mainly of men, I soon discovered that people of all genders—including trans people—were there every step of the way too. We just needed to look for them. Going back 3,200 years, we have the story of a man in Ancient Egypt who "removed his penis" and told his wife that he was now a woman like her.[1] We also largely know that crossdressing and stories where men took on female roles and women took on male roles have popped up in nearly every history and culture throughout recorded time. The story of Hua Mulan is a good example—a mythic warrior who crossed gender lines to serve their country, comfortably appearing as a man or a woman as needed. In the Edo period in Japan, there are extensive stories of people who dressed as other genders; particularly, the founder of kabuki theater famously crossdressed to the point where statues of her depict her, in part, as a male samurai.

And in the Western world, a short-lived emperor of Rome, who was assassinated at just eighteen after they led a four-year reign of debauchery and overturning of sexual mores in Rome at the time—quite the task—was also fond of dressing as a woman, insisted on being called a lady instead of a lord, and actively sought out sex reassignment surgery, according to contemporaneous histories. Elagabalus, as they were called, delighted in being called a lady and a mistress of powerful men, and offered money to any physician who could provide them with a vagina. They were assassinated in the year 222 CE.[2]

In the Americas, Native tribes commonly have a third gender or two-spirit designation for trans individuals. This designation existed well before the Americas were colonized by Europe and Native tribes were subject to assimilation and genocide. Colonial historians wrote of Iroquois women who took on male roles and seemed to become men and of men who became women within their tribes. This switching up of gendered roles among Native people seems to have been quite commonplace and was understood and accepted as a normative practice prior to colonization.

But the colonies themselves had people who exhibited what we now identify as transgender identities. Most famous, perhaps, is that of the Public Universal Friend, an AFAB evangelist who, in 1776, reportedly died and then resurrected as a genderless androgyne who preached a gospel similar to common Quaker theology. They refused the use of gendered pronouns and wore androgynous clothing throughout their life. Their clothing was a traditional black clergy robe, under which feminine petticoats peeked out, and a traditionally masculine brimmed hat paired with traditionally feminine scarves. They called themselves Public Universal Friend, which companions at the time respected, referring to them as The Friend or simply P.U.F. When interlopers inquired about their gender or manner of dress, they would simply reply in a style mimicking biblical text: "I am that I am." The Friend was considered a great evangelist of their time; they moved out to western New York and helped settle two towns there where many women were empowered to take on traditionally masculine roles.[3] The settlements were largely an attempt at a utopian society to embrace the coming of Christ and preached not only equality in gender but celibacy. Property was not held in the name of The Friend but rather through a board of trustees.

The Friend was not without trial, however, as they were frequently accused of blasphemy, largely due to newspaper reports that embellished or outright fabricated claims, such as that The Friend was claiming to be Jesus Christ. At one point, these accusations even ended up in court, where a judge ruled that, in the newly adopted Constitution, a separation of church and state meant that the court could not and should not rule on blasphemy cases. This case set a precedent for future separation of church and state rulings, continuing to influence the court even today as it debates questions of religious freedom as a mechanism for discrimination in businesses that serve the public.[4]

As a result of the furor over The Friend's claims about themself and newspaper accounts also functioning as a rumor mill, a lot of biographers disagree about The Friend's role in the early life of the New World colonies, many placing them as a woman who took on the role of a man in order to subvert traditionally male roles of preaching at the time. However, contemporaneous accounts of The Friend's refusal to be called by gendered pronouns—neither he nor she—and desire to be referred to simply as The Friend indicate that their life was not an exercise in female empowerment but rather something else entirely: non-binary before we had the words for it. The Friend's identity was also fairly biblically rooted as in Galatians, the apostle Paul writes that there is neither male nor female in Christ, and it's entirely possible that The Friend took that verse quite literally and *became* neither male nor female in practice.[5] This matches with The Friend's own narrative that they were embodied by a "genderless spirit" and existed as a tool of G-d's work on earth rather than as a person confined to a specific role bound by space and time. As such, when The Friend passed away, members of their Society said that they had "left time"[6] rather than saying that they had passed away or died.

The Friend was also not the only person who saw the flexibility of gender within the Bible. Numerous trans scholars, like my friend Austen Hartke, have written extensively on the topic. Hartke writes in his debut book, *Transforming: The Bible and the Lives of Transgender Christians*, of how the Bible sets up binaries but that those binaries do not disallow for the in-betweens. After all, we still have dusk and dawn, beaches and marshland, hot, warm, cool, and cold. Hartke proposes that what Jewish writers are laying out in Genesis is not a binary but more of a spectrum that covers all possibilities.[7] G-d created the land and the sea and the beaches and the marshes.

Many scholars also point to the existence of eunuchs in the Bible as an example of the variants of gender. In other neighboring cultures at the same time, eunuchs were considered a third gender that passed between man and woman and did not fall into the specific roles that twenty-first-century evangelicals see in the text. Evangelical Christians like to use proof texts to argue against trans people, like Deuteronomy 22:5, which reads, "A woman must not wear men's clothing, nor a man wear women's clothing, for the LORD your G-d detests anyone who does this." But Talmudic scholars past and present interpret the verse as an admonition to avoid being confused with cults that worship other G-ds, which refutes the idea that it is about trans people. There is also the interpretation of Rashi, a Medieval French rabbi,[8] who framed it as an admonition against pretending to be a woman to go make out with women who are not your wife (apparently that was a real problem at the time, what with communal bath houses and all).[9]

Most crucial to our Western, twenty-first-century contexts, however, is the fact that transgender identity is not a new phenomenon. To read current media talking about it, you'd think trans people invented themselves in the 1990s and suddenly burst onto the scene. Indeed, in 2020, a book came out based on the idea that trans teenagers are a brand-new phenomenon. *Irreversible Damage* invokes the specter of a moral panic, pearl clutching about the "new trend" of AFAB teens identifying as trans men or as non-binary. Abigail Shrier, the author, claims wildly that "before 2012 . . . there was no scientific literature on girls ages eleven to twenty-one ever having developed gender dysphoria at all."[10] To hear Shrier tell it, it wasn't until the last ten years that anyone who happened to be a minor expressed gender dysphoria—an odd claim, considering that "gender dysphoria" wasn't the accepted scientific term until 2013 with the publication of the Diagnostic and Statistical Manual Number 5, which changed the diagnosis from "gender identity disorder."[11] But

Shrier is not the only one. J. K. Rowling, a fifty-five-year-old writer in Scotland who was the world's first billionaire author following the massive popularity of the Harry Potter series, wrote in a post on her website in June 2020 of a "new" phenomenon affecting young people today and comments that she herself may have been persuaded to transition back in the '80s when she was a young woman. Her argument for that seems to largely be that there is a new world of transgender ideology that is perversely preying on young people and that trans men in particular largely did not exist prior to this "new wave."[12]

But one must always remember: just because it wasn't visible to you doesn't mean it didn't exist. Susan Stryker, a trans scholar and queer theorist, wrote a book considered a definitive history of transgender identity in the United States, walking us through the existing literatures and history of the trans movement. Stryker points to the 1850s as a central shift in transgender history. She writes that the shift to urban centers and the growth of cities meant that people who ordinarily would've been trapped in rural communities where they would be harshly judged for what was seen as a moral failing were now finding homes in cities, where the anonymity allowed them to fully exist as they were.[13] Stryker points out that in the 1850s, communities began to see a rash of dress code laws, a response to the growing communities of gay, lesbian, and trans people in urban centers. Back then, there was no real distinction in the queer community between different "types" of queer, largely due to how homosexuality (a term coined in 1869) was viewed. As Stryker summarizes, "Homosexual desire and gender variance were often closely associated; one common way of thinking about homosexuality back then was as gender 'inversion,' in which a man who was attracted to men was thought to be acting like a woman, and a woman who desired women was considered to be acting like a man."[14]

It's important to understand that gay, lesbian, bisexual, and transgender as static identities did not exist in our language until the twentieth century, but they *did* exist as things people *did* or began to build identities around in the nineteenth century.[15] It's well known that Oscar Wilde was flamboyantly gay, and many artists and poets in the period of the late nineteenth century into the twentieth were known to have same-sex trysts. It's only appropriate that trans people would be wrapped up in that view of homosexuality as they simply drew to the logical conclusion the inversion thought of by society: a woman who loved women might become a man as a mechanism to complete that inversion and appear straight.

It is in this time that a man named Magnus Hirschfeld began his studies. Hirschfeld was one of the first scholars of gender and sexuality as an emerging medical and psychological field in the early twentieth century. Hirschfeld was a gay man and a physician by trade and became interested in studying homosexuality after many of his gay patients took their own lives.[16] Because he saw the depression caused by the inability to rid oneself of either homosexual desire or social constraints that prevented living one's desires out, Hirschfeld began to advocate for the rights of sexual minorities and, alongside that, gender minorities. He developed a taxonomy of homosexuality and coined the term "transvestite," which was then understood to explain the identities of what we now know as transsexuals or transgender people.

In 1919, Hirschfeld opened the Institute of Sexual Research (Institut für Sexualwissenschaft) and began to compile one of the most deeply sourced libraries of research—medical, sociological, and psychological—on sexual and gender minorities. The institute was a center of advocacy for sexual and gender minorities, normalizing the existence of both gay and trans people and exploring the medical science behind these identities.[17]

The institute became an important gathering place for not only the queer community but the straight and cisgender one as well. School classes came to the attached museum to learn about sexuality, and people from all over Europe visited to learn more and seek medical consultations. It was a well-regarded fixture of Berlin's queer scene at the time, a place respected by straight and gay alike. Hirschfeld became a worldwide celebrity, touring America promoting the idea that a more open view of sex could improve straight marriages, and spoke out for the independence campaigns in India in the 1930s. But the institute was short lived.

In the 1930s, the far right gained control of Germany's government and began cracking down on what they saw as deviant and criminal displays of sexuality. Adolf Hitler was appointed chancellor of Germany in January 1933, and by May of that year, the Nazis sacked the institute, piling the library of research in the street and burning it. University students who were members of the Nazi party assaulted staff, and Berlin police declared the institute permanently closed. Hirschfeld himself only escaped violence due to the fact that he was overseas on one of his tours to promote his research. He was exiled to Paris, hoping to eventually return to his beloved Germany, and worked on finishing a book on theories of racism and "racial wars." Hirschfeld died in exile in 1937 and thankfully never lived to see the depths of horror experienced by his beloved community—both Jewish and queer—in World War II.

I tell all this history to demonstrate a couple of points: first is that transgender and gender-variant people have long existed and are not a new phenomenon. And second, our history as a queer community has been erased through brutal acts of violence and suppression. The reason many think trans people are a new thing is not solely because of ignorance; it is because we have been violently removed and silenced, kept out of the narrative and unable to tell our own stories. Trans people had to develop their own support networks, constantly fearing the outing of themselves as different and the potential punishment of the state for living their truth. Urbanization and concentrations of populations made it easier to hide, to disappear into the crowd, to become just another face, but this did not necessarily protect us fully, as the destruction of the Hirschfeld institute demonstrates. The LGBTQ+ community lost centuries of research and the archives of our kind to the violence of fascists, which has allowed others to rewrite our history to remove us from it entirely.

To properly and accurately discuss trans identity and trans formation, one must understand that it includes a history of being erased, excluded, and violently removed from history. Trans people have always existed; their presence in the community is not a new thing. We know that because some transgender people were notable enough that history actually wrote about them, which means there were many, many more with quiet lives who lived and died in communities without anyone ever noting their existence in the historical record. People who insist that trans people did not exist when they were growing up are simply demonstrating their ignorance. Trans people existed before the theory to explain gender did, just as straight and gay people existed before we had the terms "heterosexual" or "homosexual."

So what we know is that theory did not create the transgender identity—it merely describes it and seeks to understand it further. There is no more an argument *for* the existence of trans people than there is an argument for water feeling wet: it is a law of the universe, and what remains to be seen is how we as a culture respond to the increased visibility of transgender people. What *has* changed from past cultures is the ability, now, to respond medically and to treat gender dysphoria with medical interventions. This scientific progress has raised the profile of transgender people, creating anew the debates around who should access treatment and what ways medicine is a gatekeeper toward the realization of embodiment. This has made the idea of identities outside of cisgender seem brand new.

But that is not the reality. A German trans woman named Dora Richter had her testicles removed in 1922 and then underwent a successful vaginoplasty in 1931, around the same time that the Danish trans woman Lili Elbe was undergoing similar surgeries in Dresden. Richter is one of the people presumed to be killed by the Nazis in the sacking of the Hirschfeld institute in 1933. Even prior to that, in 1917, an American trans man named Alan Hart, a tuberculosis specialist, had a full hysterectomy to relieve gender dysphoria, which was successful. Hart then received hormone therapy when synthetic hormones were invented and made available in 1920.

Even America, cast in conservative histories as a paragon of sexual morality, especially in the 1950s, was taken by storm with the story of Christine Jorgensen, a US GI who served in Japan at the end of World War II. After the war, she traveled to Copenhagen and came back, as newspapers called her, "a blonde bombshell." She toured the nation, advocating for the humanity of transsexuals, and wrote a best-selling autobiography about her life and transition. Her work contributed to the humanization of transgender people in America during that time, moving them out of the category of "freaks" and "perverts" to people who were perceived as "normal," just different. This advocacy came at a time when feminists were coalescing in the women's liberation movement, and the civil rights movement was burgeoning in the American South. Jorgensen lived until the 1980s, continuing to advocate for transsexual Americans and pushing forward movements for transgender people to be allowed to change their sex designation on their birth certificates and undergo name changes.

My parents were both born in 1951, around a year before Jorgensen's story took over the news cycle. My father is now in his seventies. It is impossible for anyone living today to say that trans people are somehow a new thing. Those who turned one hundred in the year this book publishes grew up in a world where trans people were not only visible, but they received medical care to better conform their bodies to their own identities. It is simple reality, not some new paradigm brought on by a cabal of doctors and gender ideologists.

In the 1960s, the University of Minnesota here in Minneapolis was the second hospital in the nation to begin offering vaginoplasty for AMAB transgender individuals. In December 1966, the university publicized that it was going to begin surgeries in a planned ten-year longitudinal study of trans patients and how surgery affects their quality of life. The news appeared on page 1 of our state newspaper, the *Star Tribune*, alongside an article by Lewis Cope, a staff writer at the *Minneapolis Tribune*, arguing that surgery "can mean 'life or death' to patient."[18] The article went into detail about what transsexuality is and how transitioning can improve quality of life for individuals.

Over the next two decades, as the archives of the *Star Tribune* demonstrate, reporting on transsexual individuals was commonplace, with most of the articles simple, straightforward reporting on the success of the early operations, often stating how the surgery was largely beneficial to the patients involved. In November 1972, in fact, an article on how full transition and acceptance results in improved outcomes for trans patients appeared on the front page, above the fold. The headlining story took precedence over a report on peace talks in Vietnam involving Henry Kissinger.

It is only after 1980 that the tone of the pieces begins to shift, which can be attributed to two elements: first, Dr. Renee Richards, an ophthalmologist who began transitioning socially in college and later received vaginoplasty in 1975. Around the same time as her surgery, she started playing tennis at a professional level, competing in women's brackets, sparking up a now-familiar argument about trans women athletes competing against cisgender women. Richards was outed as trans by San Diego reporter Richard Carlson, the father of the infamous television host Tucker Carlson, and the US Tennis Association required her to undergo genetic testing to compete against women. Richards challenged the case in court and won an injunction that finally allowed her to compete in 1977. Richards never reached a rank higher than 20 on the national circuit and never even won a tournament as a singles player. But the controversy over her case meant that trans issues were now fraught topics for newspapers, and the articles about trans surgeries seem to have lost their objective tone, now noting the controversy of such surgeries.

In addition to the Richards controversy, Janice Raymond's *The Transsexual Empire* came out in 1980. Raymond's book is perhaps the bible of the transphobic feminist sect, arguing that transsexualism undermines women's rights and, most famously, claims that "the issue of transsexualism has profound political and moral ramifications; transsexualism itself is a deeply moral question rather than a medical-technical answer. I contend that the problem of transsexualism would best be served by morally mandating it out of existence." Raymond herself went on to explain this quote in a follow-up on her website: "What this means is that I want to eliminate the medical and social systems that support transsexualism and the reasons why in a gender-defined society, persons find it necessary to change their bodies."[19] This book was popular among lesbian separatist feminists at the time, and it influenced a great deal of the discourse around trans bodies that continues today.

—

How we remember the past shapes our future. The stories we tell about ourselves as a culture reflect not just who we were but who we want to be. A historical record that erases the contributions and presence of the queer community as an active participant in the shaping of society is one that sees no place for queers in the future, either. Embracing and understanding the past, both in academic theory and in historical record, is vital to not wasting our time repeating the same arguments and mistakes well into the future.

But, of course, cultural memory only extends so far, so it is not surprising to me that we are debating these same things as my parents must have in their time. Cultural acceptance ebbs and flows and, unfortunately, with it, the civil rights that ongoing cultural acceptance can afford. In 1993, a young trans man by the name of Brandon Teena was murdered in the small town of Humboldt, Nebraska, almost a straight shot south on Interstate 29 from the town where I grew up. Teena's death created national headlines, led to discussions about hate crime legislation, and caused many newspapers to declare the cultural moment as a first glimpse into the struggle that trans people in America face.[20] But, of course, as C. Riley Snorton points out, this was not the first glimpse: just forty years before, Christine Jorgensen had returned from Copenhagen to massive publicity and headlines across the country.[21] And, as Snorton lays out, even the memories and conceptions we carry forward into the future about the trans community have the ability and tendency toward erasing the impact that whiteness and anti-Blackness have had on our cultural memory. Brandon Teena did not die alone. With him was Lisa Lambert, a white single mom, and in the next room was Phillip DeVine, a Black man who was an amputee below the knee on his right leg. In retellings of Teena's story, DeVine has been sidelined and erased altogether (he does not appear in the movie adaptation *Boys Don't Cry*).

Snorton discusses DeVine's life and develops a "biomythography," attempting to piece together what little is known about DeVine and refuting the idea that he was simply in the "wrong place, wrong time" when it came to his murder. In doing so, Snorton seeks to right the wrongs caused by the racial politics of memory, where narratives get cut apart and cleaned up and straightened out to tell a simpler story of martyrdom or heroism, often casting aside the implications of anti-Blackness in telling a queer story. The specific anti-trans animus that led John Lotter and Thomas Nissen to murder Teena after he was outed as trans by the local sheriff intersected with their anti-Blackness, leading them to also murder DeVine, who was one of the only Black people in town at that time. DeVine's memory sits alongside and intermingles with trans histories, creating upon those who read history later a burden to include and examine all portions of the historical narrative—not just those that have been made into neat and clean martyrdoms or heroics set in place by biographers with unexamined anti-Blackness in their construction. This examination is part and parcel of our cultural memory—our decisions about who belongs and who doesn't—and who gets erased from the record.

—

When I moved into a new apartment in 2017, I became curious about the neighborhood, knowing it was one of the older areas of central Minneapolis and therefore carried with it the lives and histories of those who had come before. I looked up my building in the county register and found it was built in 1912. The tenement house had stood through two world wars, through riots and civil rights movements. It had narrowly avoided the scarring cut of the construction of Interstate 94 as it connected Minneapolis and St. Paul and the suburbs. I found myself looking at old maps of the area, wondering about the Sunday services that happened at the church that used to be across the street, now replaced by the whir of cars along the interstate. On the other side of my place sits one of the oldest gay bars in Minneapolis, with no windows facing the street and a large hidden backyard a monument to the lives of the queer community in the past, when the community had to hide its gathering for fear of police raids. And I found myself lamenting that finding such histories would be constantly and consistently complicated by who has chosen to remember them and archive them.

In France, with the advent of social media and children becoming famous online before they can even navigate the touch screen on their own, they have passed a "right to be forgotten" law. A child, upon reaching adulthood, can request that sites take down images and posts about them made as minors, allowing any cataloging parents did for social clout to fade into the distance, dropped from memory like so many parts of our past. This law turns on the idea that record-keeping is vital to keeping a memory alive, that we remember histories more readily when we have primary sources from that time, and that an individual has a right to disappear into history if they want. This can be crucial to members of the trans community, who want to rid themselves of their dead names and old images, burying who they were thought to be and resurrecting again with new life as the person they are. In some ways, we all deserve the ability to be forgotten, to have our old mistakes expunged, to be pardoned in public opinion and understood not as the person we were but the person we now are.

But we also crave, as humans, for our memory to live on. We have children, build families, and maintain histories so that someone, down the line, will know who we were. Many in the queer community have a chosen family, arrived at after many of us were rejected by our biological families by coming out for who we are. We aim for that sense of community because it means something to us when someone else knows us for who we are and for who we want to be. That type of companionship comes with the security of memory—the assurance that when you are gone, you will be remembered by someone, somewhere, and that they will miss your presence.

Perhaps what we need for the queer community is a right to be remembered, a protection for us against those who would erase us from our own histories, who would black out our names and burn our books. It is our history, and we have a right to tell it and to continue to contribute to it. Who we are as a people depends not just on what we do now but on our pasts and how we learn from them to change the future. It is not enough that we remember the past within our community in the here and now but rather that we create a record, a trail of crumbs so some future generations can know where they came from and who we were.

This book, this work, is my trail of crumbs, a documentation of who I was and who I am seeking to become. I write not only to show my past self who I can be but to show the future community this moment in the debate, this movement toward describing who we are, a snapshot of the here and now. We, the queer community, the trans community, deserve to be remembered.

3

THE THEORY OF US

Hearken unto me, fellow creatures. I who have dwelt in a form unmatched with my desire, I whose flesh has become an assemblage of incongruous anatomical parts, I who achieve the similitude of a natural body only through an unnatural process, I offer you this warning: the Nature you bedevil me with is a lie. . . . Heed my words and you may well discover the seams and sutures in yourself.

—Susan Stryker, from her performance essay "My Words to Victor Frankenstein above the Village of Chamounix"

When I was working on my first book—a polemic against the hetero- and cisnormative "ethics" of evangelical purity culture—I knew that I had to cover the idea of transgender individuals and how their identities differ from those of cisgender people. In particular, in talking about reproductive rights, I wanted to be clear that cisgender women were not the only ones concerned when it comes to legislation around uteruses. I deliberately used "they" pronouns through that chapter to ensure that I wasn't excluding trans men and non-binary AFAB people from the narrative.

Then I got the copy edits back and discovered that my copy editor had changed every instance of "they" in that chapter to "she." I nearly had an aneurysm. So possessed was I by this egregious misreading of my text that I completely missed that in other spots, the copy editor had redacted the space between "trans" and "woman," rendering the term as "transwoman" and, in other places, removed the asterisk from after "trans," as writing "trans*" was the fashion of that time for the inclusion of any gender-nonconforming individuals. Calling trans women "transwomen" tends to render them as an Other by rendering their identity as a noun rather than simply an adjective modifying the category of "woman."

Years later, I'm still annoyed about the "she" thing, but I'm fairly grateful that she removed the asterisk in parts, because it wasn't long after publication that the asterisk fell out of favor with the community. But the idea behind the asterisk remained: the trans community is wide and inclusive of any person who experiences discomfort with their assigned gender at birth.

The asterisk is taken from computer language to mean that "trans" is a prefix that could be affixed to any number of words like "-sexual" or "-gender."[1] It was meant to signal that the trans community was much larger than suspected, that it included anyone who was *transgressive* about gender. This concept gave rise to the popular idea today of the "transgender umbrella." Falling into various visual representations, the idea is largely that the term "trans," now a word in itself (and without the asterisk), covers a number of identities not typically identified as trans. The list includes but is not limited to:

- Androgynous individuals
- Bi-gender

- Feminine men
- Masculine women
- Transsexual individuals (trans people who medically transition)
- Third gender
- Intersex
- Genderqueer
- Hijra
- Two-spirit
- Non-binary individuals

The idea is that the term "trans" can be used to describe any individual who is gender-nonconforming, even those born intersex, cis women who present butch, or cis men who present in feminine ways. Any kind of individual who engages in *trans*gression of gender rules counts under the umbrella of *trans*.

The idea of the trans umbrella came about as early as the 1980s and became common by the year 2000, though queer theorists were still largely struggling with where "transgender" fit into the category of "queer" at the time. Unlike the other letters of the LGBT community, the T sits alone as dealing with gender identity. Theorist Susan Stryker observed this as an issue back in 2004 as she reflected on the previous decade of queer activism being subsumed into a debate largely about "gay marriage": "Most disturbingly, 'transgender' increasingly functions as the site in which to contain all gender trouble, thereby helping secure both homosexuality and heterosexuality as stable and normative categories of personhood. This has damaging, isolative political corollaries. It is the same developmental logic that transformed an antiassimilationist 'queer' politics into a more palatable LGBT civil rights

movement, with the T reduced to merely another (easily detached) genre of sexual and gender identity rather
than perceived, like race and class, as something that cuts
across existing sexualities, revealing in often unexpected
ways the means through which all identities achieve their
specificities."[2]

Stryker herself grew up in the age of the transsexual—a
medicalized term, mentioned in the previous chapter, des-
ignating people who had undergone sex-change operations
(now called gender-confirmation surgery). History tells
us of transsexuals prior to the advent of queer theory, but
the overlap between transsexuals and the rest of the queer
community was fraught. Medicalization of the identity
meant that transsexuals often had to contort themselves
into boxes in order to receive medical care concerning their
gender identity. For most of the twentieth century, part of
the diagnostic criteria for "gender identity disorder" was
maintaining heterosexual relationships, largely because
transsexualism was considered a disorder of sexual identity, a disorder of the desires originally part of one's sexual
role. This was aided by the idea of inversion—that a gay
man is "taking on a female role" and a lesbian is taking on
a "manly" role in loving their same gender. A transsexual lesbian (a trans woman who likes women), then, was
incomprehensible to the largely cisgender male medical
community at that time tasked with treating trans patients.
Therefore, trans people who were also homosexual or
bisexual were sidelined mainly because of the demands of
the medical establishment in order to receive treatment.[3]

But in the 1980s and 1990s, queer theory, the sexual revo-
lution, and advances in psychiatry helped divide the differences between a gender identity and a sexual one, and the
inversion theory largely fell by the wayside. Underground

subversive gay culture included everyone from bears to twinks to jocks to daddies. And lesbian subculture included femme and butches and fuckbois and cottage core, and it was by then understood by the queer community that same-gender love was not merely a mirror image of hetero-sexuality but something in and of itself, something entirely its own. Femmes dated femmes, butches fell for butches, twinks fell for other twinks. Heterosexuality, with its atten-dant strict gender roles, didn't map onto homosexual rela-tionships as neatly as previous theory about homosexuality had thought.

In the 1970s, "gay" became a *political* category, an iden-tity that you are, not merely a descriptor of inclinations but a part of a person just as much as being straight is part of a straight person's identity. "Gay" formed as a political identity alongside transsexual, but the fight to see homo-sexuality as a normal sexuality, not a DSM-diagnosed deviance, succeeded far before gender identity disorder was recategorized into "gender dysphoria." By the time the early 2000s rolled around, gay people had largely won the argument that they were not a medical anomaly but rather a community with a shared identity. Trans people were and still are fighting this fight.

Chase Strangio, a trans man and a lawyer for the Ameri-can Civil Liberties Union (ACLU) (Chase uses both "they/them" and "he/him" as pronouns), told MSNBC host Chris Hayes in a podcast that a lot of this consternation over the divide between gay cis people and trans people was because, in order to gain rights, the queer movement had to become a "coherent legal subject." They expand: "And so that is very much part of the constitutional para-digm and you can really see that becoming more and more reinforced the more that the mainstream lesbian and gay rights movement, in particular, exclusive of bisexual and transgender people, was turning towards legal recognition and really assimilationist in construct."[4] Essentially, because we all live in a legal framework where "rights" are based on innate, immutable identities as determined by the state, the queer movement split into gay and lesbian, excluding bisexual and transgender, largely because the latter were seen as mutable, changeable categories based on a person's context. This, unfortunately, meant that we leapt forward in terms of homosexual rights—the right to marry, the right to even just have gay sex (the striking down of sodomy laws), and rights to privacy. But we didn't have a public understanding of trans identity that could be leaned upon as a "coherent legal subject," leaving the discussion of gender out of the equation altogether. This calculation essentially sacrificed transgender rights to the priority of gay and lesbian rights.

Stryker's 2004 argument is essential to understanding what is happening with the queer community nearly twenty years later. She saw in the early 2000s, as the queer debate became about issues like marriage equality and we suffered through a second Bush administration that used homosexuality as a wedge issue, that queer politics were being softened to be more palatable to the masses. Rather than the "we're here, we're queer, get used to it!" cries of the '80s and '90s, which sought not only equality but a radical reimagining of the public and private spheres, the 2000s gay rights movement put on a suit and tie and walked into boardrooms and watered down civil rights into the ability to marry. Because of this strategic move—to prioritize the rights of cisgender homosexuals over the rights of those who are marginalized genders—the queer movement ended up boxing everyone else in under one large umbrella, placing all "queers who are not just gay" into a small box set on a back shelf, meant to be dealt with later.

This setback has forced many gender-nonconforming people out of the queer community writ large. The face of the LGBTQ movement became the Pete Buttigieges of the world, not the Venus Xtravaganzas. And all the orphaned identities who didn't fit neatly into the boxes of "gay" or "lesbian" because their own genders didn't fit in the boxes of "man" or "woman" found themselves latching on to the next closest thing, which was "trans."

Stryker argues that this sidelining of the T forced the movement into arguing for identities as immutable fact, creating standardized categories like "gay," "bi," and "lesbian" without considering that gender also cuts across all those experiences. There are gay trans men, lesbian trans women, and bi people across the board. By ignoring the universalities of how people experience or don't experience their genders, Stryker points out, the movement has largely lost the language it needs to talk about identity formation and the relationship of sexuality and gender. Instead, we are divided into specific sexualities, with all other gender things thrown together without recourse or understanding, all in the chase to become a coherent legal subject.

Likewise, theorist Viviane Namaste (then published under the name Ki) argued in a groundbreaking 1996 essay that the ways in which cisgender gay and lesbian people had approached queer theory created a narrowing of the idea of "transgender" and acted both as a critique and a gatekeeping around what it means to be transgender. Namaste primarily critiques Butler's seeming argument that transsexuals who live as a gender different from the one assigned at birth are simply offering "an uncritical miming of the hegemonic [sex/gender system]."[5] Namaste says this particular framework, which suggest that transgender people who medically transition are simply reinforcing a binary, is a problem because "(1) It can be deployed in a violently *anti-transsexual* manner, (2) it forces a separation of drag queens from transsexuals (a division which is already quite strong within transgender communities), and (3) it prevents the elaboration of broad-based transgender politics."[6] Essentially, theoretical ideas about transgender people without engagement with their lived experiences lead to assertions in theory that do not reflect reality. Butler, for once, is wrong.

For the transgender community in the 1990s, numerous theorists, sociologists, and anthropologists write, the lived experience of the trans individual is a form of lampshading the rules-based system. By becoming what Stryker calls the "monstrous," a body surgically altered using the natural materials to create an "unnatural" formation, the trans experience both challenges the gender system and obeys it at once. It calls attention to the problems created by the rules-based system and creates an understanding of gender that both ties us to and separates from bodily performance. After all, what is a body-based system of gender if not alterable?

Anthropologist David Valentine likewise proposes that the categories into which we've so neatly forced transgender people are a major issue when faced with real, true, lived experiences. He writes in an essay that follows Stryker's in that same issue of *GLQ*, "the separation of gender and sexuality as analytic categories enabled a more nuanced (and potentially more liberatory) mode for understanding sexuality as something more than simply a tool of oppression. Likewise, in mainstream gay and lesbian activism, the assertion of homosexual identification without the implication of gender variant behavior has been essential to the gains of accommodationist groups seeking civil rights protections in the last thirty years."[7] In other words, separating out the categories can be extremely useful in nuancing the conversation, but it also created a rift where *any* gender-variant behavior was removed from the conversation about civil rights in the queer community.

Valentine's work in the 1990s was largely in ballroom culture, an underground subculture of performers who modeled different fashions in competitions and celebrated queerness in all its forms. Many of the participants in ballroom were largely Black and brown young people who frequently used the label "gay" as a descriptor to cover everything from transsexuality to polyamory to homosexual behavior. Ballroom is Gay, period.

This was, Valentine notes, a problem when it came to outreach into the queer community by social services, as these organizations required specifications that the people themselves did not naturally give. They would not necessarily call themselves transgender, though the label was fitting to what their lived experience reflected. This may have been a holdover from the times when "transsexual" also meant—for doctors and medical diagnosis—that sexuality was not a part of their experience. Trans people, for an extended period of time, were considered largely asexual or vaguely heterosexual. In a lot of ways, the convergence of gender-nonconforming people under the umbrella of "gay" or, even more vaguely, "queer" allowed them to experience both gender and sexuality in ways not allowed by establishment voices.

"The unity of the ballgoers as 'gay' people is," Valentine writes, "defined not by a distinction between 'gender' and 'sexuality' but by the conjunction of their disenfranchisement in terms of both class and racial memberships and their nonnormative 'genders' or 'sexualities.'"[8] Gender and sexuality are inextricably intertwined, as Valentine discovered in researching ballroom culture, so that the broad claim of gay was one that reads both as false to the academics who insist on a distinction between gender and sexuality and as a rejection of that academic imposition on lived experience. Gender, race, class, and sexuality all became mixed up in this environment, necessarily complicating the mechanisms by which the state demands identities be coherent and static.

It is unsurprising, then, that Valentine would be one of the primary voices that went on to define the trans* umbrella, or at least put the seeds of the concept out into the discourse. In 2004, Valentine argued that "the experiential is subsumed and reordered by the categories we use to make sense of the experience."[9] In other words, lived experiences have had a kind of mutual exchange with the academic categories, wherein lived experience has been reordered to fit into the categories—which can make invisible those lived experiences that do *not* neatly fit into those categories. For example, until we had the words for it, "non-binary" people were just subsumed into the label of "transgender," even if they didn't quite fit. Author Kate Bornstein has written that they transitioned in a binary fashion back in the '80s because it was what was available at the time, but as language and understanding grew, they realized that what they were was less binary and more just "non."[10]

In 2007, Valentine published an ethnography of the term "transgender" after spending nearly two years among New York City's transgender community and noting the ways in which the trans community developed and understood itself as separate from homosexuality. His research largely focuses on the community of trans women, as trans men were not as visible or present in the late 1990s and early 2000s as trans women were. Valentine notes that the term "transgenderist" was frequently used in the '70s and '80s to define those who identify as a gender different from that they were assigned at birth but who did not feel the need for surgical intervention.[11] It wasn't until the 1990s and the coalescing of political activism for gays and lesbians that "transgender" began to become the catchall term for gender-nonconforming people. But, as Valentine notes, this widening of the category was causing problems even then: people who lived full time as a different gender objected to the inclusion of crossdressers and drag queens under the label.[12] Valentine states that the debate between medical transsexuals and people who are merely gender variant dates back to 1998: "Some, who adopt a more radical view of gender-variant identification, argue that 'transgender' has either become a synonym for 'transexual' or renders the specificity of transexual experience invisible."[13]

In other words, the debate upon which I am attempting to comment has only grown more fierce and more mainstream in the twenty-two years since it was beginning to be discussed in trans activism. Valentine also attributes the shift in collective naming of categories to shifts in identity politics on the national stage as LGB activism became more serious and widespread—particularly in the 2004 election—while the gender-nonconforming community was left behind in favor of presenting a gender-normative, white, gay man as the standard bearer for the queer community. In response, "transgender" became the political collective: "The very flexibility of transgender, its strength as a tool of political organizing, thus makes it possible to use without specifying who is being invoked in particular instances."[14] Valentine goes on to say that the ability of "transgender" to "stand both as a description of individual identity and simultaneously as a general term for gendered transgressions of many kinds makes it almost infinitely elastic."[15] Language creates meaning, and as the community grows to wider mainstream recognition, that language plays the dual purpose of identifying the group to those outside it as a coherent, comprehensive thing and giving meaning to those in the group who are working through their identities. There's naturally going to be conflict within that tension and elasticity.

But this elasticity has, in the thirteen years since Valentine's writing, become something of a problem, as I commented to a friend who was assigned male at birth and now lives and passes as a woman (and identifies solely as a woman): "By the trans* umbrella definitions, I'm trans and you're cis because you have a gender that conforms to the social constructions of femininity and I defy categorization upon being perceived." The ever-widening definitions of "transgender" to cover any and all transgression has pushed out transsexuals who view themselves as fully one gender and who have always felt that way—even if it wasn't the gender they were assigned at birth.

So from both ethnography (the study of a specific group) and theory, we land at two different but related discussions about gender: people who experience dysphoria with their given bodies and people who experience a dissonance with the way their gender is *performed* and *perceived*. These groups also overlap in hard-to-define ways.

Right now, the queer community is in the throes of a discussion about whether or not the trans community includes trans people who experience gender as a binary and experience dysphoria. In a remarkable invention of new language, Tumblr user idislikecispeople (I Dislike Cis

People) coined the term "truscum" to refer to trans individuals who experience their identity primarily through a medical lens. The implication is that "truscum" view people who do not experience dysphoria and do not seek medical redress to resolve their identity as not transgender and therefore invalid. The opposite of this, coined by the same Tumblr user, is "tucute," or "too cute to be cis," an ostensibly more positive look at trans identity that sees being trans as a positive enhancement on a person's life, rather than a source of dysphoric pain, and not seeing medical transition as necessary to their survival.[16]

Truscum versus tucute is a unique formation of Wittgenstein's problem of the use of language again but this time in a battle over the language of identity. How can the word "trans" cover both people who do not necessarily feel the need to transition medically and those who desperately require medical intervention? How can such disparate identities exist under the same terminology? Can we be trans without transition? Right now, the legal arguments tend toward requiring medical transition to be recognized under the law. In what ways can we expand that definition or develop new terminology to talk about the wider gender-variant community?

That is the crux of this question: two groups, looking the same but dissimilar in important ways, both laying claim to the same terms, and each boxes out the other as they both seek to represent what they feel are true labels for themselves. And the debate has come to a head within the last few years as examples of trans and non-binary celebrities are coming out and making news. The idea that one can be trans without experiencing dysphoria is simultaneously a rejection of the cisnormative medical establishment that has a history of viewing trans bodies as freakish and an embrace of the idea that aligning oneself with either "man" or "woman" is more important than allegiance to this largely gender-free or gender-complex community.

As liberating as the claim of the term "trans" is for many, for others it is a millstone upon their neck because of the significant amount of pain carried along with it. Are we truly a *trans* community if we cannot hold both in love within our community? Or has the term "trans" become too fraught with connotations that sting and wound? How can we respond to the internecine fight without losing the importance of the queer community?

I began identifying as a lesbian in 2018. This was a conscious decision on my part—though I experience attraction to all genders, I primarily choose to date people who identify as women. The word "lesbian" serves a functional purpose here, signaling that I primarily understand myself as being attracted to the same gender as myself and allowing others around me to accord themselves properly. When an unwanted man attempts to hit on me, I am saying something incredibly specific when I reply, "I am a lesbian." That statement within itself means "I don't date men" and can be readily understood by most who have a passing understanding of homosexuality as an identity. This is the way signifiers function, even as agreed by most of the more radical of philosophers.

But "trans" and, more broadly, "transgender" have been widened to encompass many overlapping and yet contradictory groups. For example, in the trans umbrella, "intersex" is included as a trans identity. Intersex people are individuals born with ambiguous genitals who are then raised as a gender their parents choose. Often, intersex individuals will be forced to undergo "corrective" surgery as infants in order to assign them to one gender or the other. These individuals have often been raised with a particular chosen binary gender—boy or girl—and may or may not view themselves as that gender as they get older. Some elect to change their bodies and consider themselves trans. Others are perfectly fine with being intersex and do not experience dysphoria over their bodies. Yet both kinds of intersex experiences are automatically included under the trans* umbrella because that umbrella has come to mean "not cisnormative." This is just one example of the language being inadequate.

When I first began to question my gender and whether or not I am cis, I struggled a lot with articulating myself beyond the vague notion of "gender feels." Coming around to a conclusion on pronouns has been one of the hardest parts of this journey because I am constantly asking myself if I want to mark myself in that way. One of the concepts brought up consistently in feminist theory is the idea of the "marked" and "unmarked." It's another way of talking about what is normative—trans people are forever "marked" as different by the nature of who they are. Non-binary people likewise are marked. And making the decision on how I fit into the gender-nonconforming community involved deciding which marking felt most appropriate. "Trans" never felt quite right. I didn't experience dysphoria as such; I just was reconsidering if the label "woman" was most appropriate for me. As my gender feelings matured and took shape as "non-binary," I began to see binary trans individuals as my partners in community, as part of the entire gender-expansive community.

I spoke to a few friends who had recently come around to identifying as non-binary. One replied that they just began to feel more and more that the label of "woman" didn't fit. After a few months, they flinched whenever someone referred to

them as a woman, and it was obvious that despite perception, they lacked an affinity with the gender assigned to them
at birth. Others had actually undergone a binary transition
that they were happy with but later grew into a reclamation
of expressions of "femininity" and eventually landed back on
a non-binary "they" as an identity. Most of the non-binary
people I know were assigned female at birth and come from
highly conservative backgrounds that were simultaneously
homophobic and transphobic—a combination that can be
summed up as generally "queerphobic." Many struggled
with expressions of traditional femininity and have either
rejected it entirely or learned to be comfortable with it after
lots of work and therapy. Many identified as tomboys or lesbian butches prior to coming out as non-binary or trans, a
recently high profile trend that has brought greater visibility
to the movement of gender-nonconforming community but
was not necessarily new. And many told of figuring out their
gender identity as a feeling of homecoming, of recognizing
that which may have always been there but was never quite
realized. It is like taking off the rose-colored glasses and seeing the real world for the first time.

In doing that, though, we cannot merely sit in peace at the
deconstruction of gender. Is *transition* a necessary course
that people must undergo to be part of the trans community? I would argue that, yes, transgender identity neces-
sitates some kind of movement away from one's assigned
gender. It is not enough merely to declare that one is trans
if efforts are not taken to challenge and rebuff typical forms
of assigned gender. At the heart of non-binary identity in
particular sits a pendulum moving between performances,
creating and subverting and playing with gendered presentation in an elaborate ongoing dance. Trans and non-binary
are not necessarily in themselves static; they are constantly

in flux in relationship with culture. This, in turn, creates a problem with the idea of the coherent legal subject: because non-binary is always in flux, it doesn't meet the demands of legal coherence, which treats identities as static and immutable.

Jack Halberstam is a professor and researcher in queer theory at Columbia University and previously at both the University of Southern California and the University of California at San Diego. Halberstam transitioned later in his career and therefore had an extensive body of work published under his dead name. He has written about how he feels that "the back and forth between he and she sort of captures the form my gender takes nowadays."[17] With that in mind, I use "she" when quoting work published under Halberstam's dead name and "he" when quoting writings after transition.

Halberstam attempted to tackle these questions of the divide among trans, non-binary (then called "genderqueer" or "genderfluid"), and simply more masculine or more feminine identities within marginalized sexualities throughout the 1990s and early 2000s. Of most concern to her was the question of female-to-male transsexuals and the idea of the lesbian butch. Butches are typically cisgender women who embrace a more masculine aesthetic in their style and presentation: short hair, leather jackets, jeans, steel-toed boots. In the '90s, she published a number of works exploring the idea of the "transgender butch" and the line between someone who is actually female-to-male transsexual and someone who is comfortable being identified as a woman but presents more masculine—the butch.

This debate is also extremely relevant to yours truly as I very much identify with the lesbian butch subculture and find feminine things like wearing dresses, makeup, or high-heeled shoes to be distressing and "not me."

One thing Halberstam both struggles with and embraces in his academic work is the idea that because we are dealing in identity, categories are *necessarily* unstable. Seeking this stability might be an impossible project, but as she writes, "the shifts and accommodations made in most cross-gender identifications, whether aided by surgery or hormones or not, involves a great deal of instability and transitivity."[18] For Halberstam, in 1998, "transgender" was a new word, a new label the community was trying out: "Transgender . . . describes a gender identity that is at least partially defined by gender transitivity but that might well stop short of transsexual surgery. Inevitably, it becomes a catchall term, and this somewhat lessens its effect."[19] Halberstam foresaw the issue we're going through right now—that "transgender" as a term has become almost too loose, too all-encompassing that it no longer is imbued with communal meaning in the ways in which language is designed to communicate. Because "trans" is so loose, it describes so many identities simultaneously, creating confusion about what the differences are among people who consider themselves gender-nonconforming, non-binary, or binary trans.

Petra L. Doan agrees that the concept of a "trans umbrella" is not actually that useful anymore, describing it in a 2016 article in *Women's Studies Quarterly* as a "blownout umbrella," like those one would find on the ground after a great storm. She writes that "while it is time to discard this metaphor for queerness, there is no replacement terminology that includes and possibly shelters all the people in the vicinity of this blown-out umbrella."[20]

When I first came out as non-binary in October of 2020, my sister-in-law texted me: "Does this mean you're trans?" At first, I didn't know how to respond. "I don't think so," I wrote back. "I see non-binary as connected but different. I'm not moving from one gender to another binary gender, necessarily. I just am somewhere in between, somewhere other than 'woman.'" Part of the trouble I was encountering was this linguistic one: "trans" was now so common and so broad that, yes, I am trans if simply asked. But we must drill down into what that means. Do I need to take T to masculinize my body? Do I need top surgery? I like having a vagina, but maybe not too? I found my own identity stumbling into this tension where I was unmoored, floating in open sea at the edge of a great hurricane.

Halberstam hasn't fully resolved this tension between the terms we use and the community meanings that shift and change as the fight for civil rights comes around to the more notoriously "queer" parts of the LGBTQ+ community. But he does conclude, "Specificity is all. As gender-queer practices and forms continue to emerge, presumably the definitions of *gay, lesbian, transsexual* and *transgender* will not remain static, and we will produce new terms to delineate what current terms cannot. In the meantime, gender variance in and of itself (like sexual variance in and of itself) cannot be relied upon to produce a radical and oppositional politics simply by virtue of representing difference."[21]

In the move toward achieving further civil rights for the queer community, we cannot simply define ourselves by being "different" but rather be specific in our meanings, what forms of masculinity and femininity we want to carry forth with us into the future. We are making ourself now, and we have to find our rallying cry. To be forever within the in-between is to sit in a no-man's land between warring factions instead of establishing for ourselves a port in a storm. We must take cover in our own visions of ourselves and anchor ourselves to something, even if it is simply a sandbar in the open ocean.

4

FINDING A HOME

"I don't know," replied Dorothy sorrowfully, "but it is my home, and I'm sure it's somewhere."

—L. Frank Baum, *The Wonderful Wizard of Oz*

In 2016, I chose to take four months of my life and work for the Clinton campaign in the small town of Knoxville, Iowa. Knoxville is the county seat of Marion County, about a forty-minute drive southwest of the state capital of Des Moines. From Knoxville, I managed and organized two counties; Marion and its neighbor, Mahaska, where the county seat was the small town of Oskaloosa. These small, mostly rural towns had a surprisingly strong democratic base and party structure. The head of the state Democratic Party visited several times during my tenure there, and former senators and celebrity surrogates for the campaign—including Misha Collins of the hit TV show *Supernatural*—showed up in these tiny towns to try to energize our base to turn out the vote for Hillary Clinton. My job was not only to organize people to attend these surrogate events but also to connect with volunteers and get them to go out and knock doors and make phone calls for the campaign. In Oskaloosa, I befriended an old Catholic woman who was enthused and energetic for the Democratic Party. She confided in me one Wednesday evening that she's a lesbian and recognized me as a fellow member of the community, even though at that time I'd not talked all that much about being queer. "You're our very own little Rachel Maddow," she told me in one of the best compliments I've ever received.

She wasn't the only queer person I encountered in rural Iowa. Two of my most enthusiastic canvassers in Marion County were Gayle Snook and Cindy Pollard, a married couple accustomed to being in the news, considering they were one of the first same-gender couples married following the legalization of same-sex marriage in Iowa many years before. In another memorable instance, a young man who had never volunteered for a campaign before and was newly adjusting to being out and proud brought his boyfriend down from Des Moines, and they canvassed for us together in Knoxville.

Queer people are everywhere, I soon realized, and they had as much a commitment and attachment to their rural countryside life as the alleged conservative working-class rural voter that media narratives painted. They were a minority in fairly red, rural areas, but they'd built their own small community and were happy and celebrated in their lives as queer people.

I thought of those people again as I moved a few months later to the metro of Minneapolis–St. Paul. I could've easily been one of those rural queers, but what I realized upon returning to South Dakota in the brief interlude between the election and my move to Minneapolis was that I am not built for rural life. I stayed with my father in a small town of two thousand people for a month following the 2016 election and realized what a terrible situation I was being thrown into when I inquired about local coffee shops and he said, "Well, there's the Casey's." Casey's is a gas station convenience store common in the Midwest. They make a damn good pizza, but they are not exactly a quiet coffee shop haven where I can set up my computer and headphones and camp out with a cup of cold brew while doing my work.

The sense of relief I felt when I finally settled in St. Paul and later in the heart of Minneapolis was palpable. Here was a place that not only had employment protections for people like me but also had a massive population where my own brand of weird was not something that made me an outcast or unable to make friends as it would in more rural, more straitlaced areas. I felt free to explore with my gender, eventually finding an all-gender barbershop willing to give me the strong undercut I'd struggled to explain to rural Iowa stylists. I started carrying a small wallet again and got rid of the purse I normally kept my as-needed antianxiety medications in. I found the less and less I was perceived as a woman, the less and less I needed to carry my safety net of anti-anxiety meds, candy bars, and phone chargers with me. I was soon hopping the bus, carrying nothing more than my wallet (with ID and bank card) and my cell phone, both secured in my back pockets, not unlike a traditional man would carry them. It felt normal.

So when I finally came out to myself and to the public as non-binary, I found I didn't have to switch much about how I behaved, at least in my presentation. It was already common for me to wear a sports bra that squished down my bosom to be less visible, though as a fat person with fairly substantial breasts, they would never disappear completely. I started using "they/them" professionally, wore neckties and button-up shirts as professional dress, and chopped my hair even shorter.

By the time I hit the 2020 election four years after getting to know those lesbians in rural Iowa, I'd come into my own as a queer person in a community full of queer people. I could go literal days without talking to a straight person and could count my straight friends on one hand. So when I came out to my circle, the response was largely positive, with friends asking what pronouns to use when referring to me and largely cheering me on my gender journey of figuring out who I am.

Every so often, this acceptance was jarred back into place by encounters with people who perhaps meant well but clearly hadn't done the work. During the 2020 election, my home state of South Dakota made a very unexpected move for a state built largely on conservative Christian ideals: they voted to legalize marijuana statewide. It wasn't long before an Associated Press (AP) reporter reached out to me, as a vocal ex–South Dakotan, for a reaction. I attempted to redirect him back to people still living in the state because they'd want to be able to speak for their state, and I don't live there anymore. But he insisted on asking me how I felt about it as a former South Dakotan who'd moved to a more liberal state. I carefully explained that I attributed the victory to the more libertarian streak in South Dakota politics and that no, I would not be moving back, because I'm a queer person who needs legal protections that I don't get in South Dakota. I then reminded him that my pronouns are "they/them."

"OK, that's great! The AP is kind of a stickler about ages, so how old are they?" he replied.

I stared at the screen for a full minute before I realized what was happening. And then I burst into laughter. Here was a grown man who writes for a living not understanding that "my pronouns are 'they/them'" doesn't mean "you" no longer applies. He was trying to ask how old I am without saying "you."

A few weeks after that, Elliot Page came out of the closet. Elliot had long been one of my favorite actors, and we share a birthday a year apart (Elliot was born in 1987, I in 1986). To see them come out as "non-binary trans" was an unexpected delight that, like many other instances in 2020, brought me to tears. Here was an incredibly high-profile person, asserting a new identity, a transness without the binary. I was elated to see myself represented by someone I had always admired.

I dreaded, too, what the pundit class was going to say. It didn't take long before the infamous conservative commentator Andrew Sullivan expressed confusion at the concept of non-binary altogether. "What does it *feel* like to be 'non-binary'? If it means not a stereotype of men or women, join humanity. If it means neither male nor female, and nothing to do with either, you're a different species altogether," he wrote, questioning a person who was exasperatedly trying to explain gender theory to him in a tweet.[1] To Sullivan, the "binary" referred to was an either/or proposition, and it was impossible to understand what happened in between (intersex people have apparently never occurred to him). At the time, I responded with a glib "That's right, Andrew. We aren't humans."

But the more and more I thought about it, the more "we're something else altogether" actually rang true. What if we *are* something else? I don't mean not human but instead our own category within the possibilities of human gender?

—

One of the reasons it took me so long to arrive at my own understanding of my gender is because I was essentially raised with nineteenth-century views about gender and sexuality. Being a submissive woman necessarily meant heterosexuality, and like many queer women, I thought all women just suppressed their sexuality and had to stop themselves from staring at boobs. The language for even understanding my sexuality was kept from me—as a result, so was the language about gender. To drill down into non-binary language, we need to return to a concept mentioned back in chapter 2, inversion theory, and how it influenced how we saw sexuality and gender in the early twentieth century. Inversion theory maps a heterosexual role onto a homosexual relationship. Men who want to be with men are playing the role of the woman, and women who want to be with women are playing the role of man. This can be summed up in the question "Who wears the pants?" which refers back not only to heteropatriarchal ideas of gender roles within a relationship but to specific dress codes in the 1850s that forbade women from wearing pants, as they were "taking on" masculinity when they did so.[2]

To understand precisely what sexual inversion meant in that time period, we must understand that "sex" was largely meant to refer to the person entire—their role within a society, their position within a marriage, and their work within or without the home. One's full sexual role not only referred to the very act of penis-in-vagina intercourse, in which a woman is expected to be the recipient and the man the giver (theorists at the time even read into physical positioning during intercourse as evidence of those roles), but also spoke to the person's role in the whole of life. A woman was expected and understood to be passive, receptive, and quiet. A man, on the other hand, aggressive, bold, and forceful. Women who dared take pleasure in the sexual act evinced not only a kind of perversion for themselves but an upending of the entire role they played in society at that time.

Therefore, "inversion" meant not only that a woman or a man was taking on opposite roles in the sexual act but that they were inverting their role in society too. Historian George Chauncey, Jr. writes in the journal *Salmagundi*, "early sexology sought to justify the particular form of women's subordination to men during this period by asserting its biological determination."[3] In other words, sexual roles within a heterosexual relationship were seen as biologically determined and necessary to the correct ordering of society. As a result, a woman who exhibited unwomanly behavior—from enjoying sex to seeking sex out with other women—could not do so "without inverting her complete role."[4] A woman who sought pleasure or who sought to bring pleasure to other women was considered to be acting entirely outside her role; her entire personhood was brought into question because of her active and aggressive (as characterized by sexologists of the time) attitudes toward sexual intercourse.[5]

For those sexologists in the late nineteenth century, "sexual inversion" encapsulated a number of behaviors, from crossdressing to lesbianism to gay men to any kind of sexual perversion (fetishes, kinks, pedophilic actions). All manner of "deviance" was characterized as an inversion of the societal role designated by biological determinism in one's assigned gender. But, of course, this made for unwieldy taxonomies that lacked precision, and by 1900, sexologists and doctors were beginning to drill down and create more distinct categories for sexual behaviors.[6] In studying men, they realized that the inversion theory did not fully capture the whole of the experience for men who slept with men. Many of those men did not exhibit any other classically effeminate characteristics they expected of an "invert." And those who crossdressed did not necessarily engage in male-on-male sexual relations. As a result, doctors began to divide out the categories, narrowing sexual inversion to refer specifically to impulse, not to behavior outside of the sexual. Crossdressers were moved into a separate category altogether, which sexologists called the "sexo-aesthetic inversion."[7]

Sigmund Freud then broke onto the scene, and while many of his ideas are now considered noteworthy only insofar as they influenced fiction authors of the time (like D. H. Lawrence and F. Scott Fitzgerald), Freud did lay the groundwork for the conception of homosexuality as we understand it today. Freud argued that a person's sexuality, distinct from their alleged gender role in society, was composed primarily of two concepts: sexual aim and sexual object. The sexual aim referred simply to the preferred mode of sexual behavior (what we might now call "topping" or "bottoming" in the queer community), and sexual object referred to the object of one's desire.[8]

This caused a firestorm. The idea that one's sexual object could be separated out from one's role within society and exist entirely of its own accord gave the medical and sexology community a way in to understanding homosexuality as a naturally occurring part of human sexuality, as opposed to a will to engage in sinful behaviors. It is worth quoting Chauncey in full here:

> The growing differentiation of sexual object choice from sexual roles and gender characteristics, and the growing importance of object choice in the classification of sexuality, were reflected, albeit

inconsistently, in the increasing frequency with which the term "homosexuality" was used in place of sexual inversion after 1900. While "sexual inversion" referred to an inversion in the full range of gender characteristics, "homosexuality," precisely understood, referred only to the narrower issue of homosexual object choice, and did not necessarily imply gender or sexual role inversion. Although during the transition in medical thinking which I have described, some doctors, as one would expect, used the terms interchangeably, others distinguished them quite carefully, and in general the terminology of homosexuality achieved currency in the literature at the same time that concern about object choice was beginning to supersede concern about gender inversion.[9]

In other words, doctors at the time experienced a complete paradigm shift in which one's sexual relationships were divorced from one's gender expression. This led to a greater understanding, at the time, of the gay man, the man who could sleep with other men without giving up an ounce of his masculinity—a vision of masculinity we would continue fighting about well into the twenty-first century, but we see the modern start of it here.

But, as in all things, it was not so easy for the lesbians. Lesbians were still characterized as inversions, largely because male sexologists were the norm, and they struggled with seeing women not as a separate species from men but as another human being. Those who were in relationships as lesbians were subdivided by these sexologists into "active" and "passive." The "active" lesbian was the one who took on a more masculine role, who was dubbed the aggressor on the passive receiver of homosexual force. The passive lesbian did not so much give up her gendered role but rather subsumed it into a new role with a masculinized female partner. At the time, lesbians were even referred to as having "female husbands." Medical professionals at the time also believed that lesbianism was tied to the larger movement for women's rights, particularly the suffrage movement in the United States. Apparently, lesbianism leads to voting.[10] This was largely an ongoing consequence of the inversion theory as professionals looked to sexual and pathological explanations to explain why women would be so forthright as to demand their own rights.

Luckily, by the 1920s, doctors had wisened up a bit and shifted course, after, of course, a study was conducted on lesbians who were asked "which one took on the male part," and the lesbians responded with confusion, saying, "We don't think of it like that."[11]

This insistence on different research between male and female homosexuality meant that research on male homosexuality reached a conclusion relevant to the transgender community a lot faster than research on lesbians did. One idea, left over from the time period of sexual inversion, led a lot of theorists, doctors, and sexologists to the understanding of what we properly now call "transgender." Prior to the narrowing of the category of sexuality into that of object and desire, inversion was also thought to be a physical trait, a kind of hermaphroditism, in which inverts took on physical traits of the "opposite" sex.[12] But with the advent of psychology as a field and simultaneous advances that began to see treating the *mind* as being as important as treating the body, researchers accidentally stumbled upon an explanation for transgender identities that we still use in some ways today. By separating out the mind from the rest of the physical body, researchers began to think that it was possible that a female mind existed in a male body, which would account for some of the effeminate characteristics seen in male patients or the inverse for masculinization of female patients. This also potentially explained other forms of sexual inversion, including transvestitism or crossdressing.

I would be remiss here if I did not mention that this early sexuality was theorized and understood in the 1970s through the influential French philosopher Michel Foucault, whose theories on power and truth shaped much of our future understandings of the relationships of sexuality and gender and power. Foucault argued that sexual activity is about both power and truth. Sex is a mechanism for truth-seeking, and "perversions," like homosexuality, are the actions of those seeking truth that rejects current power structures. For Foucault, the prevalence and power of the church in the late nineteenth century led many to align their identities with that power—and with it, make monogamous heterosexuality into a virtue and everything else into a "world of perversion."[13] As a result, heterosexuality becomes a means of exercising power, and homosexuality a mechanism for pursuing *truth*.

It should likewise be noted here that Foucault's reading of the church's influence is fairly flawed, considering that numerous European countries had decriminalized sodomy as early as the 1790s, and the church had waning influence throughout what's broadly referred to as the Victorian era.[14] Foucault's analysis actually rings truer for the current state of the American evangelical church and its ongoing lust for power, which has turned heterosexuality into a prerequisite for the gospel. Nevertheless, Foucault's *History of Sexuality* had an extremely important effect on queer theorists who sought to explore how gender and sexual hierarchies replicated modern power structures and the mechanisms by which we find truth, form identities, and develop our *selves*.

As we've moved away from inversion, from the medical model of both gender and sexuality, we have realized that gender is far more expansive than ever thought before. Theorists have incorporated power analyses into their work since Foucault's prominence in the 1970s and '80s, arguing that heteronormativity actually is reflected in the identities of binary transgender people and that fighting against heteronormative and cisnormative power structures is vital to the continued existence of the queer community. But how did they arrive there?

In 2017, trans theorist Susan Stryker noted that previous queer theorists had largely positioned transgenderism as a marker of compulsory heterosexuality—that trans people were actually gay people who felt so strongly about the need to be heterosexual that they transitioned. This, of course, is an absolutely wild take that erases the existence of trans woman lesbians and gay trans men. Stryker writes, "Why must the hetero- of sexuality be grounded only in naturalized and ontologized binary categories of 'man' and 'woman' that are conceived as incommensurable, and not in some more expansive notion of difference? As [philosophers] Deleuze and Guattari have proposed: not two sexes, but n-sexes."[15] Radically, Stryker argues, instead of seeing transgender and homosexuality as varying degrees on a spectrum of deviance from the heterosexual, cisgender norm, we should instead imagine transgender as another form of embodiment, just as homosexuality is another sexual identity *just as valid* as heterosexuality.

Stryker writes, "Because all sex must be symbolized, and all gender embodied, the 'problem' of transgender identification is no different than the 'problem' of non-transgender identification: all subjectivity emerges into language precisely where identification fails. Transgender . . . is just another technical art, one more creative solution among others, for tying the Borromean knot that holds the embodied subject together."[16] In other words, because gendered performance is something affecting *all* people, regardless of sexual or gender identity, then transgender and non-binary identity is no different from the issues that plague defining what a "woman" or a "man" is. Indeed, because trans people are forced to think about their gender more deeply than the average cis person, trans people may have *more* insight.

Gender and sexuality are therefore connected together, both part and parcel of determining *who* a person is, and that determination is presented to *all people* regardless of gender identity. Cis women must still determine for themselves what a performance of womanhood would look like, just as cis men grapple with toxic masculinity and other influences that change who they are. Trans and homosexual identities are merely other, natural expressions of that personhood, of determining who we are in relationship to larger society. Rather than a pathological deviance, trans identities are instead merely another valid perception of this large play in which we are all participating, non-binary equally so. The further proliferation of varied identities and the breaking apart of the ideas of hetero- and cisnormativity also help us to dismantle power structures that prioritize the cis, hetero, white male.

As we work toward a better place for all peoples, this history of pathology, inversion, and understanding leads us to knowing that these identities are just as valid, just as real as the hetero- and cisnormative "ideals." Even for those who feel like they fit within a binary of man or woman, they still must work to decide what that gender expression looks like, as do we all. Judith Butler, Patron Saint of Gender, notes that within feminism, there are any number of people assigned female who feel distance from their gender: "They get it that they're categorized that way, they operate with the category, but that's not really how they understand themselves and it's not the language they prefer. They live in a world with ambivalence or some kind of distance from those categories."[17] Understanding and defining who we are as non-binary people opens the door even for those cis people for whom the categories chafe.

We are all participating in this project of gender. We all assess stereotypes, images we have seen, our own conditioning, our own embodiment and move forward with our natural, inborn inclinations, regardless of their origin. Like the lesbians I met in rural Iowa, we have settled into the places that bring us the most joy and the most comfort. We are consistently building and making homes for ourselves, in dresses or in pants, in apartments, townhomes, or bungalows. We are looking for a way to just . . . be.

5

BORN AND BECOMING

Miss Nancy Ellicott smoked
And danced all the modern dances;
And her aunts were not quite sure how they felt about it,
But they knew that it was modern.

—T. S. Eliot, "Cousin Nancy"

My mother was distinctly not feminine. She had short, cropped reddish hair that she dyed faithfully every six weeks for most of her life. I rarely saw her in a dress, though those did come out on special occasions. In their fifties, she and my dad got really into going on cruises and went on several throughout the Caribbean, often in the winter months. These cruises inspired my mother to buy some of the most feminine and sparkly clothing I'd seen up until that point. She had dresses where the tops were covered with sequins and intricate beadwork flowing down.

But when they'd come home and share pictures, the sequined dresses wouldn't be heavily featured. There were one or two, of course, from special dinners on the ship. But in the majority of the photos, when she looked happiest, she was comfortably sitting around in a T-shirt and jeans, sunglasses on, enjoying being out in the sun in a floating hotel.

Most young women my age had moms who helped model makeup and feminine norms for them growing up. My mother was not that kind of mom. She taught me how to shave my legs, but I learned makeup and hair in bits and pieces from more feminine friends over the years. If my mom had makeup, it was some lipstick and blush, never anything so bold as eyeliner or shadow. As a result, none of this knowledge was ever passed down to her only daughter. When my brother got married, the bride herself had to help me do my hair and makeup so I could adequately play the role of maid of honor.

Because of who my mother was and how she modeled femininity, it was no surprise that I grew up to model many of her same characteristics. I have short hair that I keep cropped, I almost never wear makeup, and I'm most comfortable in a T-shirt and jeans. I was not exactly the model of femininity prior to recognizing my own nonbinary gender identity, largely because I'd managed to avoid much of the conditioning daughters tend to receive from mothers who want them to reflect femininity.

Mom passed away in 2014 after a yearlong battle with a rare illness called amyloidosis, which you probably heard mentioned on *House, MD.* Your body begins overproducing the amyloid protein and is unable to filter it out in waste product. It essentially gums up your internal organs, attacking the heart and digestive system. Before she was sick, Mom weighed in at around 260 pounds. By the time we were purchasing her coffin, she had shrunk down by nearly one hundred pounds. She had no energy and no appetite, but I still remember her joking about not having to put on a bra every day.

By the time she passed, three days before her and my dad's forty-second wedding anniversary, we'd had the chance to talk over what she wanted her funeral to look like and what specific details she wanted emphasized. We still had numerous fancy dresses from her cruise days that the funeral director was more than happy to put her in. But she turned down all those ideas. Instead, she insisted that she be comfortable in death and others should follow suit and dress comfortably too. We buried her in a plain cotton shirt and jeans, her favorite and most comfortable outfit. I showed up at the wake in a skirt and blouse, knowing that while she didn't request it, she would've wanted me to look feminine. One of the aunts I'm closest to—who married into the family when I was in high school—loudly joked that I was the only one who didn't listen to her own mom's instruction to dress comfortably. But I knew, deep down, that Mom had felt the pressure to model femininity and felt, ultimately, that she had failed in that project for me. Putting on a skirt in that moment was a recognition of my mom's desires for me and how her daughter's effort had not matched up with motherly ambition.

I wore a dark-blue T-shirt and jeans to her funeral the next day.

People assigned female at birth are socialized to be feminine, to be pretty, to be the beauty, the grace, the Miss United States . . . wait, no, that's *Miss Congeniality*. But that movie provides an apt metaphor for how it can feel to be a woman in America today. In the event you, dear reader, are not a millennial who grew up with this movie emblazoned upon your brain: Sandra Bullock is in the FBI. She's a good agent, and is distinctly unfeminine. She beats boys in boxing workouts. She knows and teaches self-defense. She has long hair, but she doesn't know what to do with it, pulling it up into a ponytail most of the time. She is clumsy. And she is the only agent who can go undercover at the Miss America pageant to try to work out who is threatening the pageant with a terror attack. She has only a few days to transform her tactless, physically awkward self into a graceful pageant queen and convince the other women not to suspect a thing.

A woman who has embraced male stereotypes to get ahead has to be coached and refined into a beautiful pageant queen, shaving parts of herself she'd never considered before, embracing makeup and styling, and learning how to *walk* and hold her body in a womanly manner. Mockingly, the movie shows us the lie that womanhood is any one thing or any one ideal. Each of the women involved in the pageant engages in womanhood in their own way, even as they are forced to dress exactly alike and learn a choreographed routine. Bullock becomes a convincing version of the woman she was allegedly always supposed to be.

But for young people who don't have a Michael Caine coaching us on womanly wiles, exploring the world of womanhood and learning what it is and what it means to be a woman can be a terrifying prospect. We look to our mothers and older, more traditional versions of femininity and know that many of those simply don't fit our time in the here and now. What worked for our mothers may not work for us, and what works for us may not work for those who come after. Each generation reinvents what womanhood is, taking lessons from our forebears, keeping, discarding, and reinventing.

It is hard—nay, impossible—to write about alleged womanly experience without creating a universal out of a specific experience, which is the burden we face in trying to dissect gender altogether. I see feminists—particularly

American ones—trying to dissect what womanhood *means* with painstaking detail, attempting to say this or that is a definitive girlhood or even couching it in exceptions and caveats about what girlhood could possibly mean. And to many of these writers—often cisgender—defining womanhood is important, laying claim to some unique experience that unites all women as part of the same class, some same shared experience that we can all point to and say, "That is woman."

Throughout the years of coming out to myself, both as queer and as non-binary and finally as a non-binary lesbian, I've turned this problem in my head over and over. Am I just running from the strictures of womanhood into something in between, something not a man but not an oppressed woman, either? Gender-critical authors would argue that, in fact, that is what trans and non-binary people who are assigned female at birth are doing. Abigail Shrier published *Irreversible Damage* in the summer of 2020, underlining what she called a "craze" among teenage girls to flee womanhood to become men, or at least something not women. A new gender identity, Shrier argues, must be a way for adolescents, especially those socialized as women, to escape into something else. She writes, "Testosterone redistributes a young woman's fat, away from all those places that give her so much consternation—thighs, hips, bottom. That cruel pageantry of online body shaming no longer holds relevance for her. No one examines a boy's photos for thigh gap, muffin tops, cottage cheese. Within the first few months of injections, as body and facial hair begin to sprout, it'll be clear that she's done serving up her body for ridicule. She's on the boys' team now."[1]

In some ways, Shrier's words ring true to me. By removing myself from the category of "woman," I am, in many ways, removing myself from the ongoing policing of female bodies that occurs day in, day out. But I am also entering into the dangerous territory where toddlers may see me and ask, "What's that?" rather than moving past, their eyes never lingering on me for much longer than it would take for their synapses to process that a person was standing there and that person matched with their already socialized accords of what men and women are.

I fear the ridicule and honesty of children, unmolded brains just beginning to be shaped, not yet knowing tact or graceful questions. When I taught at a daycare in 2014, I tried to get the kids to dance in the gym on a particularly snowy day. I galumphed around the room, bouncing up and down and waving my hands, only to be greeted by a four-year-old saying, "Miss Dianna, you look like an elephant!" I stopped almost immediately and asked, "Well, do I?" and made an elephant noise to hide that I was pained by a child pointing out my insecurities as I was gaining weight. I felt, as I grew older and put on pounds, my curves became more pronounced, I was more obviously "woman" as my size DD breasts refused to be properly tamped down or wrangled. As I became more obviously "woman," I felt a deeper disconnect with the very idea of womanhood altogether. I wanted to wear baseball caps, flannels, and neckties. I wanted to put on Vans shoes and shave my head and get tattoos. Women can do all these things. But I increasingly felt that it was not within *my* womanhood to do those things. When I presented myself as the true deep butch I felt most comfortable as, I felt less a woman and more as a middle ground, a vague shape known just to me as "queer."

In many ways, this goes back to my life as a tomboy. After I refused to brush my long hair as a child, my grandma—a hairdresser by trade—sat me in our kitchen and chopped all my hair off, leaving an '80s mullet style that my mother could get a comb through. I was more inclined to spend my day outside, climbing trees and playing in the snow, or sitting somewhere reading a book than I was to be playing with dolls. Though dolls I had—dolls aplenty. I remember sitting them up at boxes in my room, pretending to be a teacher helping students with their assignments and disciplining the unruly kids by making the doll go sit in the corner. I don't think my parents would describe my childhood as particularly girly, given the numbers of times they rushed me to urgent care for a concussion or stitches or broke an ice pack out of the fridge to try to stop the swelling of a developing black eye. I was rough and tumble—not strong, per se, but definitely more than willing to take on a fight.

In the fourth grade, I switched schools from the one where my dad was principal to one close by my house. I could walk to school for the first time, and I was the new kid for the first time, robbed of the power of being the principal's daughter. And, I soon discovered, I had a speech problem. My Rs came out as Ws, and I was soon seeing a specialized therapist, though I had no real idea of what was wrong with me. I dearly missed my friends at my old school, an emotional opening the boys at my new school latched on to like a lizard chomping down on a nose that gets too close. "Did you go to Wenbewg?" they mocked, imitating the way I talked about my old friends and my old school. Eventually, things broke apart to the point that I had a fight with another kid on the way home from school. I got on top of him and shoved his face into the snow and then jumped up and ran. I got called out of class the next day for a talking to with the principal. Message received, though perhaps not as intended: girls aren't supposed to beat boys.

But that didn't hold me back at home. I had two older brothers, you see, and plenty of black eyes to go around. It takes me two hands to count through all the injuries I got from rough housing, including losing teeth in the back-yard pool, concussions from falling out of the car, a scar in the middle of my forehead from an ill-fated game of tag after Wednesday night church. When my brother buck-led down and started learning the cello, I ran through the house and tried to leap over it as it rested on its side in the living room. My leap was not successful, and the bridge of the cello broke off. My brother told me years later that my rough and tumbleness combined with my plummeting grades (largely because they didn't believe girls could have ADHD in the '90s) meant that I was headed for a life of crime. Looking back, it's obvious to me how so much of my childhood was just me hearing what a girl is supposed to be and going "ugh, not that."

I don't know that I ever expressed an intention or desire to be a boy. I remember long conversations where I informed my parents of my plans to change my name when I was older to something more "normal." No more names I had to spell for an adult's benefit. No more being unable to find my name on a keychain. My variation—the double N in Dianna—was unusual in a universe overseen by the neatly coiffed yet troubled Princess Diana of Wales.

But does all this toughness, this rough and tumble nature, this desire to be something other than myself, is that all necessarily seeking to escape womanhood? If I'd known earlier that there was an escape, would I have taken it?

"Womanhood" came for me suddenly at the end of my sixth-grade year, in the bathroom of the locker room before cross-country practice. I told my best friend I found a lit-tle blood in my panties when I went to get changed, and she explained in between breaths as we jogged around the track outside the school that it was probably my period. I told my mom a few hours later that evening, which was greeted with a confused look of almost horror and complete shock. I recognize now that in that moment, standing by the living room stairs in our house before Mom went to get her car keys to go buy me some pads, that what was flashing through her mind was not *My daughter is becoming a woman!* but rather worried anxiety about whether or not I would have the same experiences of my period as she had.

Mom had struggled with her cycle all of her life until a total hysterectomy in her midthirties resolved the issue. Piecing things together, it sounds like my mother may have suffered from a mild form of endometriosis, where the uterine lining forms cysts outside the uterus, and a person often has extended, heavy periods. She did tell me that when she got her surgery, she was having periods that were months long—a classic symptom.

But my period brought no such symptoms. I had the normal awkward teenage problems of bleeding through a test, my pad being painfully obvious through my khaki pants, and that one teacher who never gave you enough time in the bathroom to do what you needed to. With the onset, my anxiety, nascent and slightly bothersome in youth, became a full-fledged disorder, with me being unable to handle the complete quiet of the test-taking environment and struggling with anxiety attacks that sent me to the nurse's office once every couple of weeks throughout ninth grade. (It would be another ten years before I was officially diagnosed.) Other than the awkward onset of the monthly visits of Aunt Flo, becoming a "woman" didn't seem to change much for me. I had boobs, but until I was well into college, they weren't more than tiny A cups. I wore suits for my debate tournaments as my mom tried to push me into more feminine skirts and blouses. I found myself, however, much more likely to trip over the skirts she put me in than to succeed in performing in them. By my senior year, my most comfortable performing outfit was a gray pantsuit Hillary Clinton would've been proud to wear.

Most of my friends were boys, but I did connect with some girls during this time. Being deeply steeped in purity culture, I was barely aware of my sexuality, led to believe that I was supposed to like men because that's what women do. I didn't like talking about stereotypically girly stuff, instead launching into lectures about the unfairness of affirmative action (I was a conservative then; I'm sorry) and talking about the latest debate tournament my partner and I went 2–2 in. I spent the evening of prom playing card games at a coffee shop with my brother—I didn't want to go and get all dressed up if I didn't have a date to take with me. I have never once regretted that decision.

I didn't feel *connected* to womanhood any more than I felt connected to the car my mom drove to ferry me to and from school while I played my genuinely terrible mix CDs for her. Putting on clothing typically perceived as womanly was restrictive and frustrating for me. My mom had to explain to me what panty lines are and how to make sure my clothing wasn't see-through. At one point, she hauled me out of the car in front of my cousins to tell me to go put on a bra because she could tell I wasn't wearing one under my T-shirt. But such strictures felt false and imposed from the outside world rather than something that felt innate to me.

Looking back on my experiences of "womanhood," I can't help but wonder if I *am* simply trying to flee it. Being a "woman" does mean a lot of restraints are cast upon me in my perceived behavior—the fact that I'm supposed to wear makeup to work, that "professional dress" for women often means knowing exactly how to accessorize (I do not), and being a woman means holding back in a meeting because your interruption is perceived as rude and brazen, while the male coworker next to you is just "having a conversation." In some way, I've spent much of my adult life trying to expand my own conception of "woman" in ways I knew would strike at the barriers set up for so many of us. In abandoning womanhood to become something other, was I simply seeking the safer shores of male privilege?

In turning over my non-binary identity, I asked this question of my friend and fellow AFAB non-binary writer Jude Ellison Sady Doyle. Jude had come out about a month before I had and provided me with some reading material to consider as I was working through whether or not I wanted to come out. I asked them this question in a brief conversation we had on Twitter: "Are we fleeing womanhood?"

They wrote back, "I think the thing to remember is that if you were 'fleeing' girlhood you'd be heading toward someplace easier. This is harder. I don't think it's a thing anyone would do as a form of escapism."

Jay Prosser, a trans theorist, wrote in the 1990s about the concept of "home." In examining the popular queer text *Stone Butch Blues* by Leslie Feinberg, Prosser dissects the concept of "home" for the main character, Jess, who today may be considered alternately a non-binary person or a detransitioner, depending on your reading. In *Stone Butch Blues*, Jess is an AFAB person in the 1960s and '70s New York who first represents herself as a stone butch—a specific kind of lesbian where womanhood is disguised and a more masculine appearance is embraced. Jess, however, takes things a step further after, as Prosser writes, her lesbian home is disrupted by the return of men from the Vietnam War, destabilizing her sense of belonging as a butch in the lesbian community. Men have now invaded, and lesbian feminism itself has shifted into more of an embrace of the femme identity, with butch and femme pairings seen too much a reconstruction of dominant heterosexuality.

So Jess moves on and starts the processing of transition. They take T, have top surgery, and alter their appearance to the point that they are perceived as a man. They are satisfied with themselves with how they have hardened and grown into this masculine role. And then . . . they stop. They stop taking T, allowing their curves to return, and shaving off the stubble that so defined them. They commit instead to living in the in-between, to constantly being misperceived.

Prosser puts Jess's narrative in conversation with the common narrative of the binary transgender person, that of someone "born in the wrong body" whose transition has a final point and whose goal is passing as the correct gender. Contrary to the common theme of queer theory, which is that gender is at the forefront of life, continually challenged, discussed, and dissected, binary trans people commit largely to disappearing into their corrected gender, with many choosing to go "deep stealth," inventing histories for themselves and refusing to disclose their trans status. Though they will always be on hormones, they commit themselves—out of necessity for their own safety and desire to make their brains match their bodies—to finding a new home in a newly redesigned body, a home in a binary gender.

There is absolutely nothing wrong with this, as Prosser and numerous other trans theorists argue. Prosser himself is a trans man, having found a home in a male-perceived body, passing so easily that I had to google his author biography to confirm that he is, in fact, trans. Prosser speaks from the position of a binary transgender person—one who has been involved in the discourse about trans bodies and trans identities for nearly all the time there has been such a discourse in academia. And his conception of "home" provides a narrative for much of what we now understand as binary trans and non-binary identities. For the transsexual,[2] the body passing as male or female feels like home. When a binary trans person is able to look in the mirror and see the woman or man they have wanted to be in there, there is a sense of homecoming, of relief, of being welcome in one's own body. Prosser writes, "In passing, one strives to be a coherently gendered subject; in being read [ed: clocked], by contrast, one embodies gendered incoherence."[3]

Trans people who live in a binary, in the traditional narrative, are committed to passing as their gender. They abandon their assigned sex with the ferocity of an antelope herd fleeing the oncoming lion. Physical and psychic pain will not be escaped until their body is remade, reflecting what their brains have mapped onto their form. Binary trans people, then, demand an embodiment, an examination of how gender is reflected in the flesh and grounding themselves as their own subject in a world that takes them for an object. A trans woman is embracing all pieces of womanhood, developing her own story as a woman, creating a girlhood of her own. A trans man is likely doing the same with manhood—not fleeing womanhood but creating a new masculinity for themselves.

My best friend, a trans woman who speaks several languages and studies linguistics for fun, put transition and non-binary gender to me as the conflict between the ideas of "Fernweh," and "Heimweh," in German. Fernweh is a combination of the German for "far" (*fern*) and "hurt" (*weh*), which is commonly translated as wanderlust. More accurately, however, it is a "far pain," a longing for that which is far off, distant, and not where we are now. Heimweh, on the other hand, is the homesickness, the longing for the belonging of home. Non-binary people exist in that tension of between the Fernweh and the Heimweh—we are the constant traveler, finding and creating new homes along the way, occasionally returning to our original homes but sometimes fleeing them like a bat on fire.

As someone who has spent much of my life in motion, in travel, I know Fernweh and Heimweh well; when I am in the United Kingdom, I feel at home while also feeling my Americanness intensely, and when I am home in Minnesota, I long for the life I created in the United Kingdom. I am home in both but also not home in either. Prosser elucidates the concept of "fleeing" largely as recognizing an "unbelonging." For people who later come out as trans or non-binary, such change is often preceded by a deep sense of unbelonging—a feeling that you are not at home, not where you are supposed to be. And, Prosser argues, many who find themselves in between genders, in that liminal borderlands space, feel both a belonging and unbelonging at once—we are both at home and not in who we are.

The notion of "fleeing" one's gender appears to be an amalgamation of anti-trans talking points and confusion about what it means to be non-binary or trans. Professor Halberstam[4] addresses this idea in a piece responding to the above Prosser work. She argues that there is a home in the in-between, in the borderlands between genders, writing, "Transgender discourse in no way necessarily argues that people should just pick up new genders and eliminate old ones or proliferate genders at will simply because gendering is available as a self-determining practice. Rather, transgender discourse asks only that we recognize non-normative genders already in circulation and at present under construction."[5] Halberstam, in other words, is arguing that transition does not mean a flight from womanhood or manhood, nor an eliminationist approach that destroys gender altogether, but rather a recognition of and discussion about what "womanhood" and "manhood" mean. Each trans man or trans woman is making a deliberative statement in their own way about what womanhood or manhood looks like.

It's us pesky non-binaries who are the problem. Going back to Shrier, the author who wrote an entire book arguing that teenage trans men are simply "fleeing" womanhood, escaping into something perceived as "easier," non-binary and genderfluid identities rightfully confuse: "What bothers Chandler—and the reason [they] started a course of testosterone—was that everyone 'read' [them] consistently as a girl. [They] want to get to 'a more in-between feeling'—of being identified as a woman only some of the time. 'They/them' are the pronouns [they] claim—but sexless epicene is how [they] want to be seen. Very often non-binary teens seem to resist playing your game or speaking your language. They want to topple the board, send the pieces flying, rewrite all the rules, eliminate rules altogether. They don't want to 'pass,' and they don't want your categories. They are 'genderfluid'—and reserve the right to change their minds."[6] The existence of someone who would choose to feel home in the in-between, to be deliberately perceived not as one or the other but both and nothing at the same time, is wildly confusing to Abigail. These young people are, in her mind, fleeing womanhood but also in many ways embracing it by refusing to "complete" a transition.

Even trans men who identify as men who flout gender norms, such as the YouTuber Chase Ross, are too much for her: "While he could pass as a man if he wanted to, he seems to have something else in mind. His earrings, cat tattoos, flop of hair dyed every vivid shade of parrot, and nail polish all slyly nod toward the sex of his birth. Keeping others off balance seems part of the fun and very much the point."[7] In her attempt at bigotry, in arguing that Ross does not actually pass because he engages in traditionally feminine activities while presenting as a man, Shrier accidentally lands at the very point of it.

For many years, being trans has largely meant disappearance—whether by violence or alteration of the body to pass and go stealth. But as the queer community becomes much more visible than before, becoming coherent legal subjects, we are refusing to disappear and refusing to be disappeared. Instead, we exist deliberately in the middle of everything, finding a home in what we are not: we are not women; we are not men. We are in between. We are fluid. We are in the borderlands. Though I was taught and trained in womanhood, I can now discard what no longer fits, like donating old clothing to a thrift store and finding something new that suits me much better. I have eliminated my periods with medical intervention, stopped wearing makeup and dresses, and developed a sense of myself that is more at home to me as non-binary than womanhood ever was. I am in transit.

—

I've spent about the equivalent of a fortnight literally in the air. From my first trip leaving the country when I was seventeen for an ill-advised, colonial mission trip to Belize, to my time working in Japan, to my visits to the United

Kingdom every couple of years, I have managed to spend an extended amount of time strapped into an uncomfortable airplane seat, sucking down water in the dry recycled air, willing my ears to pop and adjust to the new air pressure. I'm used to spending a lot of time in transit. I've done Tokyo to Atlanta, and New York to Brussels to Mumbai. I've done Minneapolis to London more times than I can count at this point, as well as Chicago to Amsterdam on one very eventful flight when the landing gear got stuck as we went in to land and came down perpendicular to the runway, shearing off the tires and setting the plane on fire.

Flying internationally has always induced a feeling of unreality for me. From the moment you cross the threshold at the plane door and sit down, your reality shifts. You lose sense of time and space, with a little map on your screen giving you only an approximation of your location. In between time zones, you can only really know what time it is where you left or where you're landing, but you're moving so fast that time is now an indistinct blur, and at any given minute, it could change zones, pushing you forward or back another hour. Your world becomes a small two-square feet section with a small tray table and food that comes at hours strange to your adjusting body. On some flights, you change days entirely, waking up in Tokyo a full two days after you left but only having spent thirteen hours in transit. You begin to feel like the land you left is a myth: you have always been on this plane, in this spot, forever watching the world from above the clouds.

In writing this book, I spoke to my friend Reverend KC Slack. KC is a minister in the Unitarian Universalist tradition and a sexual health educator who identifies as nonbinary. They have a mop of blue hair that flops over to the side, partially covering the buzzed sides of their head. We spoke, as has been the norm in pandemic times, over Zoom in early 2021. We got to talking about what "non-binary" and "transgender" mean to us as labels, and they described themselves as "a transatlantic flight" where everything is in motion at all times.[8]

Non-binary finds a home in the borderlands, neither man nor woman, happily read as the Mindy St. Claire of the gendered world, alone in our own "medium place." Transgender, therefore, is both home and not home. For those for whom the traditional narrative of being "trapped" in the wrong body, passing and erasing the history of one's own body—going deep stealth—is a home for them. It is a final resting place, a culmination of years of work into becoming. For the non-binary, it is our desire to simply exist as a "not," as a permanently perceived Other. Our very presence calls to attention the question of gender as a given, forcing others into confusion to the delight of our trollish selves. Non-binary people are, in a sense, fleeing womanhood and manhood, but we are not fleeing to a perceived easier space or to a home, necessarily. We are fleeing to the in-between, constantly running, forever traveling but never landing, in that liminal space between destinations. I am choosing, for now, to exist in this middle ground, in my medium place.

6

QUEER POSSIBILITIES, QUEER JOY

The right to make my dreams come true
I ask, nay, I demand of life,
Nor shall fate's deadly contraband
Impede my steps, nor countermand.
Too long my heart against the ground
Has beat the dusty years around,
And now, at length, I rise, I wake!
And stride into the morning break!

—Georgia Douglas Johnson, "Calling Dreams"

My parents took us three kids to Disney World twice when we were younger, both times over Christmas break. My parents were very clear that the trip itself was our Christmas present, but there was always some kind of small present for us on Christmas morning. Being a young kid, this was my first experience with a major theme park and actual roller coasters, not the tiny county-fair kind that went around in an oval that was slightly sloped. On the first trip, in 1995, my mom took a seat on a bench outside

Space Mountain and wished us luck as my two brothers, my dad, and I hopped into line. As a nine-year-old, I was already a smart little kid, but I somehow didn't connect that the roller-coaster cars that darted out of a hole in the ceiling and quickly disappeared again above the crowd were the ride we were about to get on. At that age, I was deathly afraid of heights, and yet, somehow, I still happily slid into the seat behind my dad, buckled in for safety.

I only have glimpses of memory once the ride started moving. I remember screaming and crying and the realization that we were flying at the height of a tall building. We zoomed through dark tunnels, never having a real idea of what was coming next. The ride couldn't have lasted more than a couple minutes, but I was almost inconsolable at the end of it. I grabbed ahold of my mom as soon as we reconnected, and she wiped away my tears and calmed my panic. For the next two hours, we didn't go on any rides but instead met characters and bought souvenirs, experiencing Disney beyond the rides. Soon, my tears from that morning were forgotten, and by the time we found ourselves in Frontier Land, I was back to begging to go on rides again, eyeing the line for Thunder Mountain Railroad, which I'd seen on videotapes my parents had gotten to learn more about vacation packages for Disney (it was the '90s, OK?).

The rest of those trips remained tear-free, despite at least one instance of me getting so exhausted from excitement that I nearly threw up on the monorail as we rode back to our hotel for the night. I learned to be more OK with roller coasters and trying new things. I was a naturally anxious kid, but I also wanted to show bravery in exploring new experiences like my brother Marc, who eagerly hopped into the line for the Tower of Terror by himself and came back out raving about how exciting it was to see the doors open seconds before the mechanism let go and you dropped straight down for several stories. Convinced by his telling, I boarded the ride myself, with my dad by my side. Our souvenir picture has become a funny family story—there's Marc on one side of me, hands up, ready to go, and Dad on the other side of me, his arm wrapped tightly around my small body as I leaned into him and gripped hard, clearly terrified of what was about to happen. But unlike Space Mountain, I stepped off of that ride surprised that it wasn't nearly as bad as what I thought it was going to be. It was actually fun? And a tiny daredevil was born—I developed in that moment a sense of bravery that has followed me into adulthood, knowing now that if I took the leap and tried something, I might actually enjoy it.

A decade later, I sat in a classroom in Wycliffe Hall in Oxford, listening to our study-abroad instructors give us background on the cathedral we were about to go visit. The spire of the Salisbury Cathedral stands some 450 feet above the earth, the tallest in all of England, and we were going to go up it. Despite my love of roller coasters, which I'd learned to embrace all those years before, heights still terrified me, especially if I wasn't safely strapped into a roller-coaster car or in some kind of enclosed space. I approached our tour guide, explained my fear, and asked if there was a way I could do just part of the tour without going up to the spire. He told me there was a spot just before the final climb that was enclosed and had a bench for people to sit on if they didn't want to take the spiral staircase up. The rest of my group knew of my fear and encouraged me to take whatever option felt safest to me. When we got to that bench, my friend Joanna—who had been to the cathedral before—sat down with me, telling me she could keep me company. After a couple of minutes waiting, I turned to Jo and said, "You know what? This is boring. Let's go." I opened the door to the staircase and wound my way up, emerging on the balcony a few dozen feet below the spire, some three hundred feet above the town of Salisbury. My friends squealed at my appearance, congratulating me on overcoming my anxieties about heights. I hesitantly leaned forward, staring down toward the ground, feeling a rush of excitement as I realized just how magnificent this view was. Fears overcome, I beamed as I took a selfie with the town showing up in miniature in the background. Lesson relearned: overcoming my anxiety might just lead to something good and joyous and happy.

The first time someone used "they" to refer to me, that familiar feeling of joy coursed through me, combined with something entirely new. It took me a minute of sitting and looking at the words on the screen to realize that I was experiencing—in some ways for the first time—what it feels like to be affirmed in who I am. I had just come out and hesitantly added "they/them" to my online profiles, changing how these websites would refer to me and what pronouns should be used for me. It took less than a day before someone used "they" for me for the first time, and I felt a rush of happiness, a thrill that felt like all those times I'd taken a brave step and was rewarded for it. The roller-coaster thrill was back, but this time it arrived in a simple use of the correct pronouns and the acceptance of my community.

But I hadn't heard much about it before it happened to me. Back when I was presenting as and believed I was cis, most of the stories about trans and non-binary bodies I heard were stories of tragedy: trans women and men whose names we recounted on the annual Trans Day of Remembrance, trans men and women who were brutally killed for failing to perform toxic masculinity, and the struggles of years waiting for proper medical care thanks to gate-keeping. Non-binary people occasionally featured in those stories, mostly as those who found themselves out of work with no recourse because they came out or those who had to recloset because attempting to explain who they were was just too much. For many, trans lives are characterized by the violence we have experienced; the erasure of our selves and our stories both physical and psychological is a through line of the narrative the cis world will listen to.

But death shouldn't be our primary story. Da'Shaun Harrison, a non-binary Black activist in Atlanta, writes that despite identifying as non-binary and using they/them pronouns, they are frequently reinscribed to be male when they critique from their position as a Black and non-binary person. They write, "When you exist in a fat and Black body, that violence only becomes worse. So people grow comfortable with being transphobic towards non-binary people because the violence transgressed against our bodies has not yet been directly translated to Death—thus they cannot yet build social, political, and/or economic capital off of our lives."[1] Harrison's point is important here: much of the time when trans discourse enters the mainstream, it is tied to the specter of death, particularly against AMAB Black and brown bodies because many of these people are seen to be transgressing typical standards of masculinity. For many in the cis community, dead trans people are a mechanism for capital—they can fundraise off our lives, off of "violence prevention," without ever having to be confronted by the complicated and complex narrative of the self the trans person speaks. And the tragic violence against our community is so often the entryway into discussion for cisgender people that transness becomes associated with death and violence, which ends up dehumanizing the trans experience of joy and euphoria in being who they are and instead re-centers cisgender transphobic violence as the overarching narrative of our lives.

What's missing from the conversation, though, is that joy. We must imagine transgender identity as divorced from death, as not a life-taking force but a life-giving one. We must see and reflect the joy we experience when someone uses our correct pronouns for the first time, when the doctor responds to your coming out by correcting your chart and asking you how you'd like to proceed. We must be able to see ourselves happy, in the everyday banality of real life, to understand the whole of the trans experience.

I started out exploring these ideas in an unusual place: census statistics. I looked into the current scientific understandings of non-binary gender identity and what presently exists for calculating how many of us there are and how many of us are assigned one sex or the other. Dr. Petra Doan, an urban planning professor at Florida State University, focuses her research on the LGBTQ+ community and published an article in 2016 that argues for a widened understanding of transgender in order to get more accurate accounts of those affected by policies aimed at a gender-nonconforming or "gender flux" community, as Doan calls it. To this end, she performed a meta-study on the current numbers and understandings of the transgender community, from those using solely the medical model to those allowing for self-identification. By widening our understanding of the community to include those who may not seek transition but still present as a gender other than the one assigned at birth, Doan puts the actual estimate at either 1.1 million trans people in the United States or 9.1 million, respectively.[2] Doan also complicates the potential counts of those who are assigned male versus those who are assigned female, saying that estimating those categories is harder by and large because people assigned female at birth can "crossdress" with little to no consequence, while people assigned male often face a stigma for being perceived as male wearing "female" clothing.[3] Doan sidesteps the question, arguing that we should apply an equal percentage to both populations as the smaller community that has medically transitioned has also reached a gender parity, so we should assume the same for the "gender flux" community.

In other words, there are a lot of us out there. Nearly ten million, if Doan's estimates are to be believed (and I'm inclined to believe them). But we rarely see the representation and narratives that reflect our actual lived experiences— the joy and the pain.

Much of our understanding of the gender-varied experience comes from what gets reported out and therefore dominates the narrative. This means most of the public knowledge available about trans and non-binary lives is filled with tales of murder, death, and mutilation. We are constantly targeted for being who we are—especially trans and non-binary people who are assigned male at birth— whether it's by a particularly virulent grouping of cis women calling themselves feminists or state legislators who want an excuse to further eliminate queer people from public life. Adrian Silbernagel, a trans man writing for *Queer Kentucky*, notes that much of our lives is characterized by violent reactions *to us*: "In the US, the aspect of trans experience that doctors and psychologists and the media fixate on is *dysphoria*: the experience of discomfort, dissatisfaction, or distress over the *wrongness* or *incongruity* between the trans person's internal and external reality, between their sex and gender, body and mind, presentation and inner sense of self."[4] We are, to a cis public that simply doesn't know better, an amalgamation of suffering, a collection of the worst parts of all selves, an object upon which the worst of the world's assumptions and objectifications are wrought.

I am focusing on the way this narrative impacts those assigned male at birth because the cisnormative world we live in is interested first and foremost in preserving male access to power. Therefore, people perceived as men who then "give up" that access to power to live either as women or as something distinctly not binary inhabit this subliminal space where they are punished from all sides. They will never inhabit the female realm well enough, in the minds of their woman critics, and they are betraying something distinctly important in denying their maleness. Erin Paterson, a non-binary trans person who writes for *British Vogue*, talked about this experience of coming out:

> When I recognised myself as a non-binary person, I made sure that people knew, that people understood that I was done with my male gender. It did have an effect on the way I was received, and the way that people interacted with me. I felt the burden of expectation drop sharply and felt the confidence to state plainly the ways I would be respected. This is important for me, but it's infinitely more important for the people coming up behind me to know that this is possible, this is acceptable, and that you will still be loved. Finding a "logical family", as Armistead Maupin termed it, is a process that won't always be right the first time, because you have to find yourself first. And to find yourself, it helps to be able to see yourself in others.[5]

Paterson's point, largely, is that while they were the first in their particular workplace, in their community, they are not the last. By being who they are, they are paving a path for those who come later, who are just now feeling the flickers of thought about their gender and who they really are. Paterson also knows that they were not able to come out fully without the examples of queerness they saw in others, like Jonathan Van Ness, the beauty and hair expert on Netflix's revival of *Queer Eye*. Van Ness is a non-binary person, assigned male at birth, who wears nail polish, a full beard, and elbow-length hair. They dress themself in skirts and "female" clothing or post videos of themself dancing in nothing but their boxers as they make coffee in their kitchen. For many of us—especially for many AMAB non-binary people—Van Ness's coming out as non-binary was a watershed, a moment when we saw ourselves represented in the mainstream in ways we'd not seen before. For once, here was someone happy, successful, and fully embracing who they are, including being non-binary. Criticism seemed to roll off their back, and instead they focused on returning joy to other queer people, creating space for us to develop and court joy through their online presence, podcasts, books, and television shows.

During the writing of this book, a close friend had gender-affirming bottom surgery. Her original set of genitals was surgically altered to create a vagina, rerouting her urinary tract and removing every remaining reminder of a penis that there had been. The first time I saw her post-surgery, I gave her two boxes of Thin Mints I'd gotten her to celebrate and gave her a hug. Sitting back, I thought to myself, *I've never seen her so happy*. She had a sublime smile on her face as she unpacked the Thin Mints, pulling the first two from the roll and biting off a chunk with pure delight. It had only been a week, but she was already becoming a new person. She cracked jokes with nurses in the hospital and talked openly about how she didn't feel psychic pain every morning now.

I recognized in her what I was experiencing myself as people called me "they" and "them" and removed me from the group of "woman": euphoria, joy, pure, unadulterated happiness from understanding and being seen as truly, wholly yourself.

Erin Paterson also wrote in 2020 about how lockdown for the pandemic allowed them to embrace the aspects of transition that made them nervous, such as lipstick. They write:

> Lipstick is a particularly significant and weighty topic for AMAB trans and non-binary people. . . . I'd worn it on a few Zoom calls, spent hours gazing at myself in the mirror and oscillating between feeling ridiculous and stunning. But, one morning, when I was wearing a mood-boosting raspberry hue, I decided that I felt beautiful, and I was heartbroken at the thought of removing the lipstick to go and get my shopping. The overarching feeling was one of self-betrayal: I felt like I was re-closeting by going back to what I had had to adhere to in order to survive in society.[6]

They reached a point where not living their authentic self was more potentially devastating than the risks from outsiders who didn't believe in their right to gender expression. They experienced a rush of joy as they stepped outside, in public, with lipstick on for the first time. In that moment, joy overrode any anxiety, any fear at being visibly queer.

This is one of the reasons representation of differently gendered or ungendered bodies is so deeply important: seeing ourselves reflected in the public not only gives us courage to be who we are, but it also asserts for us that it is right and normal and OK for us to feel *joy*. And it's OK for us to want that, to want to live a life free and open and joyous.

In February 2021, eleven days before I turned thirty-five, I went out for the first time fully dressed as *myself*. I'd gotten a pair of fancy blue dress shoes that resembled wing-tips. I ordered a navy-blue men's shirt from Amazon and bound my chest down to resemble that of a fat man instead of a well-endowed woman. I put on my favorite tie, a pink cotton one with little blue feathers falling gracefully down it. And as a nod to the temps that were below zero, I put on my pair of extra-warm gray jeans. As I was walking to check my PO box at the post office downtown, I noticed I had a spring in my step and I stood a bit straighter. I had done the brave thing. The roller-coaster feeling was back. I felt *good*, and I felt like this was who I was meant to be this entire time. The new shoes pinched as I hadn't broken them in yet, and my ears burned from the cold wind, but G-ddammit, I felt at home in my body for the first time in ages. I was performing my gender in the way it matched in my mind—a dapper non-binary person with softer feminine features but a dress and bearing that read as masculine.

I don't know how other people I ran into that day read me. The lady at Starbucks who had helped me the day before (I have a bit of a habit) told me to remind her of my name, so I wasn't completely unrecognizable. But I didn't have a problem giving her my feminine name because it is part of who I am, and honestly it was fun to present masc but still hang on to some femininity. I felt like I finally hit that in-between where people had to guess.

And this ultimately is what queer non-binary people of every stripe need: we need more of us visible in the world, happy and at home in who we are, honest about both our suffering and our joy at being able to be who we are. We don't always get it, because we live in a binary world that insists on putting us in boxes, especially if we have

traditionally gendered markers like facial hair or prominent breasts. But the closer we get to being able to experience life fully and on our terms, the better living is for all
of us.

—

My friend Flan (pronounced like "plan") Park also asserted
the importance of *play* in our non-binary lives. They are a
genderqueer library worker in Philadelphia and are active
in leftist politics, particularly union-organizing movements. They describe themselves as non-binary largely
because they recognize the political utility of that identity
but also see themselves as a "masculine woman." Their
gender heroes are the butch women who seem to be trying something different with gender roles, challenging and
changing and confusing with their presentations that deliberately skew masculine while maintaining femininity. For
Flan, this image is representative of the non-binary person
they want to be.

   When they first started exploring their identity, it was
communally, with a sense of play to their ideas; their
name, Flan, comes from a Twitter joke where they chose
to represent themselves with a custard emoji, which eventually became a nickname and then a name in its own
rights. Being with a queer community that not only nor-
malized pronoun-giving but also understood that gender
identities are not always static and require both introspection and outward affirmation was immensely helpful for
them as they determined who they wanted to be. They also
recognized the importance of simply modeling different
genders both inside the community and outside it. "Gender is expansive," they argued in an interview with me in
February of 2021. "Sometimes you end up just spinning
in circles inside if you don't have a chance to express it or

experiment or play around with it."[7] Making the internal visible externally is vital for all non-binary individuals.

Erin Paterson writes in a different article (also for *Vogue*) about the importance of non-binary representation: "When I came out, I realised the importance of feeling seen as non-binary, of being received as a person who was neither strictly male or female. It's important for us to be welcomed as we are—and ultimately, it's damaging when we aren't."[8] Being received fully as who we are, not as women who wear ties or men who wear dresses but people who inhabit the in-between, the middle, reaffirms our identity and brings a euphoria at being really truly seen. And, Paterson writes, a major part of this need for representation is showing joy as much as showing real sorrow.

Dr. Helana Darwin, a sociologist at SUNY Stony Brook, approached this issue in the presentation of non-binary gender, especially for AMAB people, in her paper "Doing Gender Beyond the Binary" in 2017. In it, she creates a virtual ethnography of non-binary and genderqueer persons by examining more than five hundred threads on the subreddit r/GenderQueer. In it, she found a multitude of opinions about what "doing gender" looks like outside a binary and a lot of consternation about whether or not non-binary people can lay claim to the label of transgender. But perhaps most importantly, Darwin found that much of the discussion focused on how non-binary people visually convey their gender in a world bent on gendering them within a binary. She writes, "Again, it appears there is no one answer to this question, given the diverse gender identities within this sample. Some wish to evade binary gender attribution in keeping with their [genderqueer] or androgynous identities; others wish to 'pass' as one gender on one day and another on the next, in keeping with their 'genderfluid' identities; and others do not feel a need to visually convey their non-binary gender at all."[9]

This diversity of approach means there's often no one *look* to being non-binary, which further confuses the cisgender world about what and who we really are. One AMAB writer in the subreddit is quoted by Darwin as saying, "I personally try to achieve a lot of 'center of center' effects by picking articles of clothing that cross a gender boundary away from my assigned birth sex (male), but then somehow do it in a way that 'comes back' towards it. Examples would be, I often wear an outfit with skirts or leggings, but then the color scheme would be drab earth tones, more typical of colors men tend to wear."[10]

For many of us in the non-binary community, visibility is itself a major stumbling block, as many of us seek to find ways to demonstrate outwardly the complexity we feel inwardly. This pressure appears to be more significantly laid at the feet of AMAB people because those markers that allow a visual claim to non-binary gender (e.g., facial hair) are often also sources of dysphoria. So AMAB people who identify as genderfluid, non-binary, or genderqueer end up in a concerning position where they are both hypervisiblized as symbols of the non-binary community and erased as individuals with differing experiences. This creates a unique tension for AMAB non-binary people as their accountability to a cisnormative gender model is more highlighted as distinctly nonconforming and therefore open for punishment. And that punishment will often come in the form of denying the AMAB person's access to a gender of their own making altogether.

This came up when I spoke with my friend Max Malament, a genderqueer person who lives in Colorado. Max initially transitioned as a trans man; they found it hard to navigate their gender identity in a world that didn't have examples of genderqueer people who were ground in masculinity but sought for expansive conceptions of that masculinity. They actually delayed transition due partly to toxic masculinity: "I saw these representations of what men were in my family of origin, and what men were like in my church of origin, and I even saw men like Buck Angel . . . body builders [who were] my examples of trans masculinity. I'm not like that. I don't see myself like that. I don't wanna be like that." This is a pressure I've noticed as well, as a masc-of-center person who is soft and squishy and not at all a "bodybuilder." There's a pressure for men, trans or otherwise, to be considered "tough" and "muscular." Along with that comes immense pressure to reflect the worst of the toxic "manly man" imagery, and such pull is understandable. It erases all doubt about one's manhood when you are embracing things our culture has deemed "masculine."

The non-binary AMAB person is also fighting against toxic masculinity in a lot of ways. They purposely eschew the idea of "passing" as any other gender than what they are, often embracing a presentation of the genderfuck—the person who deliberately refuses to be read as one gender or the other as a mechanism to overturn ideas about gender signaling altogether. In doing so, they are upending toxic masculinity, putting bodies visibly read as male into outfits and fashions that toxic masculinity calls "demeaning" for men to do. They paint their nails and grow their hair out but keep a thick beard. They shave their legs and wear dresses one day and put on a flannel, but only half buttoned with a cami on underneath, the next day. They take male fashion and add in traditionally female signals to it: wide-brimmed hats, overlarge glasses, lace and camisoles and heels. They deliberately, purposefully, fuck with gender in ways that are often more visible and available to them than those who are AFAB—precisely because toxic masculinity is so strong.

And when we win that fight against perception, there's a lot of joy to be had, not only for non-binary people but for your cis friend who wants to paint their nails or be perceived in less traditionally masculine ways. Breaking down the closet doors for some of us leads to the breaking of those doors for all of us.

Trans theorist Sandy Stone wrote in the 1990s that trans bodies exist as a "set of embodied texts whose potential for productive disruption of structured sexualities and spectra of desire has yet to be explored."[11] In other words, trans people change and affect the discourse around "what is a woman" and "what is a man" largely through allowing themselves to be read as texts with full, complicated, and complete lives rather than invisibilizing themselves in "passing" as the "opposite" sex. It seems, then, that non-binary people are doing what Stone says must happen in order to shift the discourse: refusing to disappear into normal.

AMAB non-binary people, in themselves and in their existence, offer more visible challenges to this discourse because masculinity has, by and large, been given a static, stable position within society's understandings of gender. Their presence in the community complicates and problematizes cultural narratives about the non-binary community existing largely for "women" who are "uncomfortable with the role of womanhood."

Being non-binary is a source of queer joy, of experiencing the world as more fully ourselves and telling our stories without the strictures of toxic masculinity violently enforced. Our own cosmology is not too dense to navigate—it is just different from what other people would tell us to be. As Kate

Bornstein put it in a piece for the *New York Times*'s celebration of Pride 2019, "When it comes to gender and sexuality, I am nothing but possibilities. What's more, it turns out that these days I've got a non-binary family: lots of people who are neither men nor women. All of us are virtually nothing in the eyes of a culture that sees two and only two. . . . That's a whole lot of nothing going on, and it makes me positively giddy to think what that might mean for the future."[12]

7

FAT, REDISTRIBUTED

You do not have to be good.
You do not have to walk on your knees
for a hundred miles through the desert, repenting.
You only have to let the soft animal of your body love what it loves.

—Mary Oliver, "Wild Geese"

My mom and I delighted in shopping together throughout my childhood. She loved going into Target and looking at all the home goods and storage ideas, imagining how organized and beautiful her shelves and rooms could be. It never quite worked out, thanks to three unruly children and a husband with undiagnosed ADHD whose organizational preference seemed to be simply piling things in different categories on the floor. At one point when I was thirteen, my mom admonished me to go pick up my room by pointing out that I had a literal path on the floor between piles of mess.

"It's a *big* path!" I defended, only to be turned around and given the afternoon to clear it up.

But shopping for clothing was another beast altogether. Instead of being a pleasant wander through possibilities, trips would often turn into fights, with my mom picking up a feminine shirt or blouse and me rolling my eyes and going, "Ugh, no one wears that" as though my mother, who was born in the 1950s, would be hip on the fashions of the 2002 teenage girl. A sign of the teenage fights started up when I began, according to my mother's metrics, "needing" to wear bras. I was five-foot and some inches on a rail-thin frame, but the forces of puberty had caused little A cups to show up. Confused by the idea that someone would *need* any more coverage than what a T-shirt gave, I barely participated in the bra-buying experience, responding "I guess?" to every training bra my mom held up as long as it didn't have lace or flowers. When we got to the checkout, I looked up and loudly asked, "Why do we need bras anyway?"

The checkout lady giggled, while my mom blushed red and explained that for many women, their breasts bounce around, and we need to sort of lock them in. I looked down at my own insubstantial chest and went, "Oh." I wondered what that would be like, if my breasts would eventually grow into something more substantial. They did, but by that time, I was beginning to question their presence altogether. As I grew up and my body reached a homeostasis above two hundred pounds, I found myself having to shop in the plus-size bra section, where bras that kind of sort of fit correctly cost seventy dollars or more for one.

It didn't take long before I found myself cursing my chest daily. Shortly after coming out as non-binary, I bought myself a binder for the first time. Putting it on was a struggle, but I practiced at home, putting it on for about twenty minutes at a time, watching my chest contort and flatten out. My shirts buttoned, and I squealed with delight when I realized. But I found myself inspecting my body under the shirt, aware that no matter where I shoved them under the material, my breasts were still there. The first few times I tried it on, they formed an uncomfortable ridge that made it feel like my breasts were directly under my chin. After trial and error, I learned to pancake them flat against my chest, pulling them more in line with my belly fat, and soon my chest simply resembled that of a fat man.

Physicality has never been my strong suit. When I was in middle school, I ran track and cross-country, forcing my gangly teenage body into smooth loping motions across the field, never quite understanding that you shouldn't slow down and wave when you see your mom in the stands cheering you on. In high school, I discovered the debate team and poured myself into four years of refining my research and rhetoric skills, gaining confidence in putting together evidence and following politics to understand arguments about "political capital" and "weak or strong markets." Debate introduced me to Foucault and elements of critical theory. I already enjoyed spending most of my time in books and in my own head, but debate honed my critical thinking and, best of all, didn't require me to wear a sports bra.

Ever since I gave up sports for the more stimulating challenge of debate and eventually parlayed that into a writing career, my relationship with my body has been tenuous at best. It didn't help that for much of my twenties, I was plagued by an undiagnosed anxiety disorder that caused my body to rebel in embarrassing and frightening ways. I bolted from movie theaters, thinking I was going to throw up, and found myself crying on my living room floor as I struggled to breathe following a panic attack. It felt like my body was betraying me at every turn, robbing me of the ability to simply sit and listen in a meeting without feeling like I was going to die from panic.

But now, my body poses a different problem. My panic is (largely) under control. I've got a pretty set style and idea of how I want to look as someone in my midthirties. But I also am deeply aware of how large and intrusive my body actually is. I sit in an airplane seat and tell myself, "You can't get any bigger, or you'll need to buy two." My breasts, by now into the cup sizes beyond D, announce my assigned sex well before I open my mouth. I *know* I'm non-binary. But, culturally, we don't really have images of non-binary people who look like me. Fat bodies seem to both be degendered and regendered in feminizing ways. Fat men have "moobs" or "man boobs," marking them as "female" in the cisnormative world. Fat women likewise are degendered, no longer seen as sexual objects, especially if they, like me, lean butch and choose not to engage in feminizing performances.

Aubrey Gordon, the creator of the website and blog Your Fat Friend, wrote an incisive and vital book in 2020 about fatphobia and how fat people experience the world, called *What We Don't Talk about When We Talk About Fat*. Weaving statistics and science together with her own experiences of fatphobia, Gordon makes the case that fatness is another vector by which oppression occurs—and she doesn't restrict her findings just to other fat women like her. In a section addressing how fat bodies are desexed and degendered by their perceived lack of desirability, she writes that "our cultural imagination seems to cast fat trans and non-binary people as failures in two rites: failures to embody the thinness that is expected of everybody and failures to uphold a binary understanding of gender as hypermasculine or hyperfeminine. . . . Not only are fat trans people desexualized, the very narratives of their own bodies are wrested from them, too."[1]

As I scrolled through non-binary Twitters and TikToks, I rarely saw bodies like mine represented. Thin, white, waify teenagers flaunt in front of the camera, demonstrating the ease with which they slipped between genders, wearing a corset one second and flipping around into a blazer and a tie the next. Ziggy Stardust to the Thin White Duke to Jareth all in a sixty-second span. Where was *my* fat, bisexual alien goblin king?

To address the problem of the androgynous ideal we've created of non-binary identity, we must first address the attendant expectations we have, culturally, of androgyny. In my research, I ran across Dr. Francis Ray White, a researcher and lecturer in sociology at the University of Westminster in London. They write candidly—for an academic—about the experiences of being fat and on the transmasculine-leaning edge of non-binary in a way that I saw myself reflected: "For myself, as for many on the transmasculine spectrum, a flat chest is a powerful marker of non-female-ness, one that tantalizingly seems to promise a life free(r) from incessant misgendering, or in other words, from the painful everyday erasure of one's gender identity."[2] But as fat people, both White and I wonder simultaneously if a desire for ridding ourselves of the most obvious signifier of womanhood is a betrayal of body acceptance and fat acceptance politics as espoused in fat studies.

Fat studies develops a conception and understanding of fat bodies and fatness as a stable identity within culture, examining the ways in which fatness interacts with gender, race, class, and, in particular, ableism in varying ways. Fatphobia as a form of oppression is central to the idea of fat studies as an academic and activist arena.

White points out that the primary conflict between fat studies and transgender studies is that they both land upon the body with differing conceptions of the self. The fat activists proclaim we must learn to love our bodies as they are, reimagining what "woman" or "man" look like to fit fat bodies into those ideas. Transgender studies, on the other hand, proclaims that our bodies and our minds may be in conflict and that to resolve that conflict, it may be necessary to physically alter the body. It is hard to explore acceptance of oneself as a fat person while also feeling the sense of unbelonging that transness or non-binary identity brings to the fore.

I'm largely accepting of my body—I used to be thin, now I'm fat, and this is how it is for nearly everyone in my family. My father was a stick-thin cross-country runner until he married and settled down, giving up running and most physical activity for raising kids and living in the suburbs. My mother was likewise a conventionally thin woman until the stability of marriage and three pregnancies widened her hips and handed her a double chin. Part of embracing my fat body was recognizing just how much it made me look like my mother.

It makes sense to me, then, to accept my body as it is, as the fat size 20 hips and jiggly belly it possesses. And yet I long to wear button-ups with a flatter chest, wanting to look more masculine and more easily read not as a woman, not as a man, but something in between. And if I could lose weight in the process—maybe not to the point of being a waif but to the point of simply being read as "on the thinner side"—it might not be bad either.

I had to ask myself why this felt like an ideal image of non-binary identity to me: a thin, typically white, androgyne, where you look at them and wonder, one who truly

brings up the question "what are they?" in the cisnormative mind.

The first non-binary person I knew in real life was a
coworker at a nonprofit I worked at here in Minneapolis.
Dana was a wispy AFAB person fond of wearing all black
to accentuate the dark black mound of curls on their head.
Dana and I shared a cubicle, as the only two queers in the
office, and I found myself a bit jealous that they were immediately read and obvious as a queer person, while I had to
carefully calculate coming out and emphasize myself as
queer by being unafraid to mention my girlfriend. Dana's
delicate features, pale whiteness, and thin androgynous
frame made their non-binary identity obvious and acceptable to the cis people in the office. Their presence emphasized my distance from the androgynous ideal, even as I
dyed my hair and shaved the sides of my head and wore
more masculine clothing.

But as I took on more visibly queer, visibly butch presentation in my own life, I found myself disappointed that my
body didn't allow for bending and changing as easily as it
would've ten years ago when it was one hundred pounds
lighter. My fat softened my features, preventing the hard
masculine jawline that would really make my shaved undercut pop. I constantly compared my image of myself to the
images of non-binary identity I saw represented around me.
Thin, white, androgynous people who could flit easily from
masculine to feminine with a simple outfit change and a
shave. I put off recognizing my own non-binary identity in
large part because I had to work through accepting my own
largeness first.

Dr. White is correct to point out that fat acceptance activism is built upon accepting bodies as they are. No one but
me and my doctor needs to know anything about my body

and my health or lack thereof. But gaining acceptance in the trans/non-binary movement made me feel like I had to shed these parts of who I am so I could adequately present as the confusion, the in-between, the masc and femme in one body. My body became a barrier to my embodiment rather than a path toward it.

Realizing this was an eye-opening moment for me: the reason I felt so uncomfortable in my body and in my gender identity was because two goals were in conflict within me, like two wolves fighting over a single chicken. I wanted to flatten myself out, to see my body as androgynous, to force others to question their immediate gendering of me. And I wanted to grow comfortable in my own body, accepting my fat and my jiggles and my curves as part of me and part of my legacy as the child of my mother. I realized that my primary goal of seeing myself as androgynous would mean a reexamination of what it means to be non-binary.

"Non-binary" emerged as a term in both academic queer theory and internet culture, which leapt ahead of queer theory's ideas about trans identity in its attempts to explain trans people's own selves to a cisgender, uneducated world. Up until around 2007/2008, it was common to refer to anyone who resisted their assigned gender at birth as trans. And it's an argument that makes sense—to be trans simply means to "cross over," to travel, to leave a home behind and create a new home elsewhere. Any gender-nonconforming person was thus caught up in the label of "trans," as discussed in chapter 3. But following the publication of David Valentine's *Imagining Transgender*, and the advent of a greater trans visibility throughout online communities, discourse took it upon itself to define the different parts of the trans community, laying out the cartography of the trans world.

One element of the landscape became eminently clear over the years of back and forth on trans inclusion and identity: there are multiple different ways of gender transing, of traveling through gender lines. There's the binary, the traditional narrative of transgender identity we have been taught, which used to be called "transsexual." This has since become known as "binary trans." That is, binary trans people are those who feel they are women who were assigned male at birth and men assigned female at birth. They go from one end to the other, inhabiting a fully realized maleness or femaleness, however that is imagined.

Once we had the "binary," "non-binary" was an easy leap. This became the collective term for those who fall into the middle of the spectrum, who consider themselves neither male nor female. "Non-binary" emerged as a popular term around 2012 and became accepted in academic literature around that time as well.[3] People who previously identified as "genderqueer" or "genderfluid" came under this new grouping. Their identity is characterized by movement, by the playing with of gender on the stage they've built for themselves. They're female-presenting one day and male-presenting the next or taking up both all at once.

This highlighting of the travel, through the Fernweh and Heimweh, conflicts with the conception of the fat body as a static identity that should be accepted as it is. Fatness is something that just *is*, making a non-binary fat identity harder to conceptualize because it means both accepting your body and rejecting it at the same time. Our cultural understanding of non-binary, however, lacks bodily acceptance and discussions of the ways in which fat lands upon the gendered body.

In the years since "non-binary" became the popular and accepted term, the images of it we have been presented with are largely those people for whom slipping between performances and identities is as simple as combing their hair in a different way. They have angular features that can be read as masc or femme depending on the day. They are frequently white and thin. If AMAB, they are bearded with long hair, and with a simple application of lipstick, they assert a femininity that challenges and confuses the cis observer. They can perform genderfuckery with ease.

But I can do none of these things. Once an image has been created of an identity, members of that community are made to feel uneasy and left behind by the cultural perception of who they are. The non-binary identity has culturally come to mean traditional androgyny, reinscribing old ideas about gender into a new form, focusing again on image and reception instead of inward feeling.

Such images are the only ones deemed acceptable to the white cisgender gaze. Androgyny has always been read as a somewhat masculinized thinness, but it has also been read as white and Western. It was European colonizers who brought the concept of sex as a binary into Native cultures. In the United States, many different Indigenous cultures have held space for a variant gender identity, now collectively called two-spirit. How that functions as a concept, though, is heavily dependent upon the Native culture using it.[4] It came into use in 1990 as a way to translate an array of Native traditions for the dominant culture but means an immense number of things to different tribes. Often, it is analogous to our non-binary gender, but not always, as many Native tribes do not construct gender in the same ways we do. Additionally, because of the force of colonialization, narrowing down those routes and meanings is immensely difficult and problematic, thanks to ongoing colonization of the academic field of Native studies by non-Native whites who claim to have Native heritage.[5] Author Ma-Nee Chacaby cowrote a book in 2016 about her journey as a two-spirit lesbian and spoke to the Canadian Broadcasting Company about how two-spirit people were treated when white colonization happened:

> My grandmother said, you have two spirits in your body, mind, soul and your heart. She says, you're going to have a hard life, a real tough life because of who you are. You're carrying two spirits, and people don't want to understand that. Then she said, way back, seven generations from the time she was a little girl, she had been told that there were two-spirit people that lived among First Nation people and nobody ever made fun of them. They were regarded as special people. They didn't make fun of them that way, she said. Now it's like this because of what we're told we are. We are told we are savages, and we are nobody except if we join the other people.[6]

Because of her two-spiritedness and her identity as a lesbian, Chacaby, who grew up in Ombabika, a First Nations reserve in Ontario, Canada, found her life to be difficult when working with people outside her Ojibwe-Cree community because they could not comprehend her differences.

In Western, cisnormative, heteronormative society, cisgender people are far less likely to recognize gender identities or roles from minority cultures, in large part because we have so deeply ingrained ourselves into the white images of gender dimorphism and "acceptable" variance. Bodies are policed by this white supremacist vision into normative beauty ideals, with androgyny only allowed to be a very narrow, thin slice of the whole of gender presentation. Social pressure—reproachful stares, "helpful" comments, deliberate or accidental misgendering, and outright hostility—all work together to enforce a white, westernized vision of gendered bodies upon the individual.

Aubrey Gordon writes eloquently and evocatively about the times she has faced the policing and concerns of strangers. In one memorable encounter, a woman in a grocery gently plucked a melon—a cantaloupe!—from Gordon's cart and instructed her that she didn't need any more sugar.[7] While reading Gordon's account with rage and horror, I recognized the judgmental stare she described, the silent policing fat bodies encounter in public, especially around food. And in my increasing desire to be "read" as the in-between, I see the judgment intensify when I am at once fat *and* unable to be gendered immediately. When I wear my binder out in the world, flattening out my chest, every so often there is a double take, the suburban mom at the Container Store glancing at me sideways as I pick up a new olive oil dispenser, the man on the bus looking me up and down, trying to assess what or who I am. When you're entering the public sphere as non-binary *and* fat, your body becomes a Rorschach test, a presentation for public commentary.

Max Malament has been a friend of mine for a decade now, despite never having met in person. Even so, our friendship stretches across the years, through breakups, new relationships, new identities, and the growth of our careers (Max in nonprofit, mine in writing). When I first met Max through mutual friends on Twitter, they were just beginning their journey into medical transition, documenting taking testosterone for the first time. At the time, they identified within the binary as a trans man. But as they've grown more comfortable with who they are, they've returned to a non-binary identity, though they prefer the more general "queer" or "genderqueer" as labels, partly because being a "not" doesn't read to them as correct. Max has also struggled with a restrictive eating disorder for much of their life, first emerging prior to transition.

The prevalence of eating disorders within the trans and gender-expansive community is horrendously undercovered. Members of the trans and gender-expansive community are more likely to experience disordered eating: somewhere around three in four of us have either had a disorder or currently have one. But, Max points out, much of that is hard to explain in terms of body image alone: "There's a lot of overlap, because a lot of us have childhood trauma, too, and that's a known trigger,"[8] they told me in an interview in early 2021.

I grew up being warned about eating disorders. We watched poorly produced, sanitized-for-school dramas about the dangers of eating disorders. On the high school oral interpretation competitive circuit, there was an ongoing joke that the drama category was "rape and anorexia world." But despite all the popular culture obsession with eating disorders, scientific study into what causes them and how best to treat them is woefully inadequate. When I was in high school in the early 2000s, the moral panic of the day was teenage girls and eating disorders. "Pro-ana" communities online were the big scare at the time—communities where young girls with anorexia would gather to share tips about stopping hunger and hiding symptoms and about foods that would fill you up for the least calories. While I have never suffered from disordered eating, I was a very thin teen and was frequently accused of needing to eat a sandwich or subject to worried recriminations from aunts at the Thanksgiving table. After all, I was a skinny, white teenage girl—just the demographic prone to developing a disorder.

But the narrative is far more complicated than too much photoshop or too many skinny bodies praised, Max tells me. Though the eating disorder preceded Max's transition, it was always a part of it. For Max, who is AFAB, stopping the monthly cycle, a serious symptom of severe anorexia, was a huge draw, and it was actually in treatment back in the late noughts that they realized that the root of a lot of their disordered eating was actually gender dysphoria. They wanted to disappear their female form, to present more masculine, to *be* masculine while still embracing femininity. They wanted that in-between, that queering of gender, that liminal space that fucks with a cis person's perception of who they are. Before medical intervention, the eating disorder was a homebrew mechanism for dealing with dysphoria, a form of extreme body modification. And wanting to rid oneself of dysphoria through changing our eating can sometimes seem, to a brain desperate to understand its housing, like a completely logical conclusion.

Trans people in general have complicated relationships with our bodies, and mine is no exception. As a teenager, I struggled with embarrassing acne and desperately wanted to change the shape of my nose. When I looked in the mirror, I had endless critiques for myself—I was too skinny, too gangly, yet somehow broad-shouldered. My head looked weirdly small for my body, and I couldn't figure out how to dress myself well (to be fair, late '90s and early 2000s fashions were not exactly kind to anyone who was not a model with a flat stomach). I remember when I met up with my childhood best friend after our freshman year of college, she commented that it was nice to see me taking on the freshman fifteen and looking less like I was steps away from hospitalization. I learned, after years of comments like that, that people were going to have their opinions about my body, and it's probably best for me to ignore them at all times. That conception has only gotten stronger as I've gotten older and added more pounds to my frame. This is the body I have—why listen to criticism of people who don't have to live in this skin?

Reverend KC Slack put it to me this way when we spoke on Zoom: "Our bodies are in flux, and as they change, we change. Gender is in flux too."[9] As a fat person who has always been fat, KC has had to learn to view fat not as this other thing that has changed them but as a part of who they are. One of their guiding principles both as a minister and as a sexual health educator is that the body you have is the only one you get, and therefore you have the authority to either change it or accept it. No one else gets to make that decision for you, despite the fact that we have a medical establishment and a cultural establishment that say otherwise.

The medical establishment has long been one of the barriers and gatekeepers to fat people simply living their lives. For many trans and non-binary people who do want to undergo gender-affirming surgery, they are required to be at a certain weight. This isn't, as both KC and Aubrey Gordon point out, because the surgery itself is risky for fat people. It's because hospitals haven't standardized anesthesia practices for fat bodies—despite the fact that fat bodies make up a substantial percentage of the population and occasionally, like everyone else, need surgery. Fat people, cis and trans, are consistently being made responsible for the thin world's inability to adjust their mindsets to imagine other bodies. Another person's lack of moral imagination shouldn't preclude me from living as who I actually am—their gendered boxes don't have to apply to me.

Dr. White, likewise, proposes that fatness be reorganized in theory not as an obstacle to gender but as a corollary, as an aid to exploding our definitions. White points out in a chapter they contributed to a book about fat studies called *Thickening* that the current conception of transness has much focus on the morphology of genitals, even though hormone replacement therapy also affects a redistribution of fat into more legibly gendered spaces.[10] I was delighted to learn when I started researching binary gendered fat distributions that my particular body already mimics that of a male, with a large abdomen, skinnier legs, and a flatter behind. Using medical interventions can help readjust this reading.

One important point Dr. Francis Ray White brought up when I spoke with them about body modification and fatness was that there's a point where fatness forces a person to reassert their gender in potentially subversive ways.[11] For cisgender fat women, this often means leaning hard into the performance of femininity—of reasserting oneself as a sexual object when fatness tends to desex the body. For non-binary people, realizing that fatness degenders is at once freeing and devastating: devastating because it underlines fatness as a signal of undesire, unwanting, unattraction but freeing because it means I can use my body in any form, in any kind of embodiment, and it's totally fine because I get to gender it however I want. I get to wear goofy ruffled blouses and straitlaced button-ups, shave my head or grow it out, and it'll still be me and mine because it is what and who I am.

After my mom passed in 2014, I decided to memorialize her and her lifelong love of modernist literature by getting a *Great Gatsby*-themed tattoo. It's a large piece, covering most of my upper arm almost all the way to my elbow. Dale, my artist, designed an ornate 1920s-looking swan and set it against a watercolor lake lit by a massive green light as a nod to Gatsby standing on his dock, staring at the green light that lit the end of Buchanan's dock, where the woman he loved resides. I chose to have that imagery permanently etched onto my body because I wanted to carry my mom with me, to remember how we sat in our living room and talked about F. Scott's relationship with his wife, Zelda, and how the 1920s was an era full of experimentation and exploration. Since it was finished after four separate sessions that totaled around ten hours in the chair, I've had strangers stop me on the street to remark on its beauty, asking politely and not so politely if they can have a closer look.

Tattoos are so common now that the fact that they are a form of modifying one's body hardly even registers. My chaplain brother and his marketing-guru wife both have them. Most people I know my age or younger either have them or have plans to have them. Tattoos, alongside piercings, new haircuts, and a set fashion style, are viewed as just another choice in owning one's body and lovingly caring for it. Just as my shorn undercut and my style of button-up shirts with classic skinny ties demonstrate, my tattoos are a part of me and are part of who I am. And now, so is this fat body I have learned to love over the years. Maybe I will get top surgery someday to deal with these pesky boobs. Maybe I will shift my thinking to imagine them as "man boobs," positioning my body as a fat masculine person rather than a "woman" and its attendant judgment. Maybe I'll learn to just be who I am, no matter what.

The conclusion I have to arrive at is that it is OK for me to want to change aspects of my body to avoid immediate gendering *and* to radically accept myself as a fat person. No one else's judgment matters. Fat is, as Dr. White points out, already not the ideal for a gender, so existing as fat effectively queers our gender as it is by presenting us as gender-nonconforming.[12] Many AFAB people in fat activism have resisted this by resorting to ultrafeminine presentation that matches with beauty ideals—they are the "fiercely real" women of Tyra Banks's world. But what if we embraced the fact that fatness already in and of itself challenges ideas of gender and desirability? I, in all my fat-ness, am non-binary. I am not a woman, as society already thinks, but I am also not a man. I am a Not, and I am happy there.

8

THE EXPANSE

I am a part of all that I have met;
Yet all experience is an arch wherethro'
Gleams that untravell'd world whose margin fades
For ever and forever when I move.

—Alfred, Lord Tennyson, *Ulysses*

I was effectively homeless in the fall of 2016. Before I signed a lease on an apartment and moved up to the Twin Cities, I stayed with my brother and his wife for six weeks while they were renovating a house they'd just purchased. One agreement we had about me staying with them was that I'd provide free daycare for their infant and five-year-old kid while they worked on painting and construction to get the new house ready to move in. On the weekends, I helped paint a beautiful new gray that softened the harsh eggshell white the walls had previously been. My brother also had the idea of painting the ceilings, which were that dreadful 1980s popcorn texture. I was working on the closet when he came in, dipped a large roller brush in the tray, and slid it up to the ceiling.

Those of you who have already done this kind of renovation project know exactly what happened next. Now wet, the popcorn paint began to loosen its grip on the ceiling. On the next pass, the entire section started flaking off in big sheets, raining down on my brother in a mixture of dust and wet paint. Turns out you can't paint popcorn ceilings. They're so delicate that the slightest wetness destroys their texture, loosens their grip, and results in a snowstorm of dry cracked paint. My brother turned to look at me where I was laughing from the corner of the room. After wiping up what was left, he realized that the entire ceiling would have to go and grabbed a scraper. The rest of the popcorn ceiling came down within the hour, revealing a smooth white surface that could easily take the paint and subsequently did so.

This project of undoing gender, of exploring my identity, has made me think back on that day, the shell of what I thought was good and right flaking off to reveal that it was shoddy workmanship and easily damaged. I never really had a handle on what it meant to be a woman, so a tiny push was all it took for me to reconsider myself and the life I wanted to lead in the world. But in other ways, this identity feels extremely precarious, so easily pushed in one direction or the other, balanced carefully on the edge of a cliff. It has taken more than a decade of self-discovery and exploration to land me here, at the precipice of who I used to be and who I am now.

In 2007, I studied abroad in Oxford and met a young person my same age from Texas. They were extremely interested in German and spoke some, so we decided to take our break vacation to Frankfurt, Germany, and stayed in a hostel together. I was an overly anxious trip planner, so we arrived at London Stansted Airport a good four hours before our flight and subsequently explored every bit and piece of that place before the gate. We were bored, we were in college, and we were weirded out by the "chewable disposable toothbrushes" available in the restrooms. When we arrived in Frankfurt, my friend happily obliged me with every weird picture I wanted to take, and I indulged them in visits to different spots in the city (though we were disappointed when we discovered tickets to Cologne from Frankfurt were way out of our budget, so a day trip got canceled). At one point, we came across a shop called The Oscar Wilde, and my nerdy self, who had read *The Picture of Dorian Gray* in high school, took a picture of the shop sign and then looked in the windows to see mannequins with jock straps and romance novels with two men on the cover. It was a gay shop.

I know I recoiled in that moment. I was twenty-one, thought of myself as a straight woman, and was deeply invested in the antigay narrative of the church. I remember my reaction was something along the lines of "Oh, that's not a bookstore," loudly and Americanly on the streets of Frankfurt, followed by raucous laughter.

Fast forward to 2013. I was still friends with a lot of people from that semester abroad, and all of us had since graduated college and moved on to graduate school or new jobs or starting families. I was living at home, helping to take care of my ailing mother. I was beginning to consider myself bisexual and exploring what that meant for me. For ages, I felt like I didn't have to say anything about it because I could just stick with men. But then my mom asked me directly, and it was like a dam burst, and I couldn't keep it quiet anymore. I began to define myself as a queer woman.

Around that time, I got a message from my friend who had gone to Frankfurt with me. I was surprised because we hadn't messaged all that often, and the last time I'd seen them, we'd gone to the Alamo together in San Antonio while I was in graduate school four years before. I could see on my phone that it was a long message, so I settled down to read. They explained that they trusted me and wanted to let me know personally that they are actually a woman. This was her coming out. She told me her new name and sent me a picture of the start of her transformation. I was stunned—surprised that she saw me as a good enough friend to warrant coming out personally. But here she was, nervously awaiting my reply. "That's fantastic," I replied, inquiring about how she wanted me to use her new name in public since she'd messaged me under the account with her dead name. I never directly asked why she chose to come out to me before coming out publicly, but I surmise that even with my previous homophobia, queer recognized queer, and she understood that even if I wasn't out yet, I had become a vocal advocate/ally for the queer community, and she was taking me at my word that I was safe.

Nearly a decade later, she's left the South and lives in a city on the West Coast with a vibrant and massive queer community. She's married now and seems to be happy. And I've come out and into my full self and now fully grasp what a risk she must have felt coming out to a (at the time) straight woman whom she hadn't seen in person in half a decade. Even now, as I adjust to being out about being non-binary, there's still a catch in my throat when I realize I need to come out to someone new and explain to them that my pronouns are actually "they/them." But I, like my friend, have deliberately made adjustments to my own life to make that move easier. I moved to a city with protections for people like me. I have a friend group that is 95 percent queer identified. I have chosen a family that accepts me for who I am, uses my pronouns, and doesn't question my identity or believe it's made up.

This is part of the self-preservation that happens within the queer community. We need to know who is safe, who is knowledgeable, and who we can have a conversation with without having to explain our identity over and over again. And yet, like any community, we cannot help but gatekeep ourselves, worrying about who wants to pathologize our identities and who wants to be "gender critical." We so rarely have control over our narratives once they are released into the world—each little step or change is visible and could be used by bad-faith actors to undermine our own community. Even within the community, we are sometimes suspicious of others who might not be queer *enough* or who believe their experience should be a primary identifier for their in-group.

Even critics of transgender identity have come to notice the discussion, pointing out the different arguments and analogies we have developed to explain queer identity, particularly non-binary identity. A quick search of the notoriously transphobic UK website Mumsnet reveals a number of threads questioning "just what is *non-binary*?" On a thread asking that question, members of the website pointed out that it's "bollocks" because not everyone fits in gendered boxes, so therefore everyone is non-binary in a sense. Another replied, "There is no definitive definition of non-binary! Each person decides what they think it means then argues their point. I wish I were joking, I'm not. Identity politics is useless and divisive, it creates and supports hierarchies."[1]

To be fair, when someone is primed to reject transgender identity, they're not going to arrive at an acceptance of "non-binary" that makes sense. But this confusion has seeped into the understanding of even allies to the trans community and members of the trans community itself. When discussing this project with people who identified as binary trans and others who identified as non-binary trans, the same questions came up again and again: if non-binary is defined by what it is *not*, how do we build a community that has room both for trans people who do fit into the box of "man" or "woman" and for people who don't believe those boxes exist at all?

All of this is still a relatively new discussion in the time-line of the queer community. We've always had, as I've argued earlier in this book, non-binary and trans people around. But how those two communities interact and fit together, especially within the larger queer community, has been an ongoing question both in academics and in real-life communities.

Scholar Avory Faucette writes in her chapter in the 2014 book *The Gay Agenda* that non-binary identity frequently brings up a series of questions: "When I explain my gen-derqueer identity to someone new, starting with the sim-ple explanation that I am neither a man nor a woman, many react with confusion or fear. Eventually, talk turns to the Million Dollar Questions—do I want to live in a world with no gender? Do I want everyone to use gender neutral pronouns? Do I want kids to grow up not knowing the dif-ference between men and women?

"My answers to those questions are 'no,' 'it depends,' and 'sure why not?'"[2]

Both binary trans and cis people have asked me simi-lar questions about this: what does gender look like in a world imagined and created by a non-binary person? As someone who's been referring to the Christian Triune G-d as "they" for over a decade, I find myself laughing a little and saying, "It already was." But the question of what society we want to build, especially in regard to gender, is an important one as feminists, as activists, and as people. And non-binary identity does bring into question what it truly means to be a woman or a man and whether or not that carries any particular meaning for society.

Faucette argues that non-binary activists have something deeply important to add to the riddles of gender: "Non-binary activism brings something valuable to the table not because it eliminates or destroys gender, but because it questions the logic behind rigid gender norms, hierarchies, and the state's use of gender as an unnecessary control mechanism. This questioning benefits people of all genders, not only non-binary people."[3] By and large, non-binary people simply want to exist as something other than what society says we must be. We are not merely a "third gender," but rather our very existence challenges the idea of gender altogether, particularly in how the state chooses to define people by pressing them into specific categories of male or female. With those categories come all kinds of attendant assumptions that serve to harm people of all genders: the idea that men are strong and capable and heads of households, whereas women are somehow more nurturing and loving and therefore better suited to childcare. For people who do not fit these controlling images, to borrow a concept from Patricia Hill Collins,[4] the project of building a better society needs to be about breaking apart and questioning those images.

Patricia Hill Collins is a Black womanist author who writes eloquently about how the state develops stereotypes to force people into boxes, particularly evident in the Jim Crow era when images of Black women as mammies and Black men as scary rapists served to reinforce white supremacist hierarchies. Simply put, "[Controlling] images are designed to make racism, sexism, poverty, and other forms of social injustice appear to be natural, normal, and inevitable parts of everyday life."[5] The idea that "man" and "woman" have specific stereotypical images attached to them is one way in which a white supremacist patriarchy catalogs people and determines them to be worthy of protection or not. Collins talks about this as part of the project of creating an Other, with the African American woman existing as the ultimate "Other" against which all other classes define themselves. Definitions of people groups and the mechanisms for how we interpret the world inherently require binaries wherein one subject—an identity that creates itself—sits in opposition to an object—a thing for which identity has been defined by its relationship to others.[6] These binaries—white/Black, male/female, straight/gay, cis/trans, and so on—necessarily depend on the othering of the one whose identity was formed in its relationship with power.

Collins also points out that these binaries are inherently unstable—subordination relieves the tension but only lasts so long. The object will always resist its definition by people in power and will always rebel against the labels cast upon it. These "hierarchal bonds . . . mesh with political economies of race, gender, and class oppression."[7] In other words, the denial of words that are our own has long been a strategy for objectifying and oppressing those in minority groups along intersecting lines of oppressions.

Throughout the twentieth century, we saw these images proliferate about both the queer community and the black community. In the 1970s, outspoken homophobe Anita Bryant, a gospel singer and orange juice spokesperson from

Florida, dominated media cycles, accusing homosexual men of recruiting young men in schools to the homosexual agenda, painting gay men as pedophiles in waiting, ready to corrupt innocent children. The gay community fought back against her ideas with a unique campaign: across the nation, queer people came out to their families, demonstrating that they are your siblings, parents, friends, and coworkers and not some scary cabal somewhere (this campaign also included urging gay people not to drink orange juice as Bryant's family was in the OJ business). Studies have since proved that a person is more likely to deny the controlling image about a marginalized population if they have someone in their life from that particular group. But that hasn't stopped people from trying.

In 1990, documentarian Jenni Livingston (who uses they/them pronouns) offered another image of the queer community with their examination of ballroom culture. At that point, the only ways in which many cisgender, heterosexual white people encountered ballroom culture was through the colonized gaze of artists like Madonna, who popularized the ballroom act of voguing in her song "Vogue." The documentary *Paris Is Burning* introduced to the world a subculture of a mostly Black and brown and extremely queer community. *Paris Is Burning* gives the rest of the world a glimpse into the ballroom subculture in New York in the 1980s. It follows members of different houses as they talk about their lives, reflect on their position in society, and explain the particular language of their subculture. The act of documentation of their lives made previously unseen queer people into subjects who defined themselves and knew their position within the hierarchy of oppression and spoke out against it. Images of "getting out" of the struggle, images of fashion are understood and subverted as images of whiteness. One of the documentary's subjects, Pepper LaBeija, summed it up in a monologue:

> This is white America. Any other nationality that is not of the white set knows this and accepts this till the day they die. That is everybody's dream and ambition as a minority—to live and look as well as a white person. It is pictured as being in America. Every media you have; from TV to magazines, to movies, to films . . . I mean, the biggest thing that minority watches is what? "Dynasty" and "The Colbys." Umm, "All My Children"—the soap operas. Everybody has a million-dollar bracket. When they showing you a commercial from Honey Grahams to Crest, or Lestoil or Pine-sol—everybody's in their own home. The little kids for Fisher Price toys; they're not in no concrete playground. They're riding around the lawn. The pool is in the back. This is white America. And when it comes to the minorities, especially black—we as a people, for the past 400 years—is the greatest example of behavior modification in the history of civilization. We have had everything taken away from us, and yet we have all learned how to survive. That is why, in the ballroom circuit, it is so obvious that if you have captured the great white way of living, or looking, or dressing, or speaking—you is a marvel.[8]

Many critics, including bell hooks, objected to the documentary as reinscribing the objectification such communities exist to defy, particularly in how the film talks about whiteness as a thing to which these queens aspire. This tension, this struggle, is part of the controlling image: that people recognize their objectification, resist it, and, at the same time, use who they are to subvert and imitate the oppressor. Capturing whiteness, as LaBeija summarizes, is not necessarily becoming the colonizer but instead passing as someone outside of this underground they have been shoved into. It is a redefinition of the self in the face of great oppression.

These controlling images and our attempts to subvert them as a gender-expansive community are central to the project of this work: defining who our community is and is not in the face of oppressions. In 2020, anti-trans feminists, under the auspices of "protecting women and children," won a court case in the UK High Court arguing that under sixteens need a court order to access puberty blockers. Thankfully, in September 2021, the English Court of Appeals overturned the decision, stating that the original High Court decision was "inappropriate."[9] But the lawyers who had brought the suit declared their intent to go after the UK's much broader standing precedent, the Gillick competence standard, declaring that the test is "no longer fit for purpose." Such threats not only would undermine the ability of trans kids to access medical transition but could possibly destroy the ability of cis girls to access abortion, contraception, and other necessary services.[10]

But much of the motivation for the original suit can be traced to the narratives about trans and non-binary people going back years. Trans women, feminists in the United Kingdom have long argued, are simply men in dresses who are predators. Despite the lack of evidence, this particular image has taken solid hold in the mainstream UK press. Journalist Katherine O'Donnell pointed out in an article for Yahoo! News that the prevalence of this narrative is largely the result of a mainstream press that tends to land center-right (and therefore promotes anti-trans voices more often than trans ones) and a state-sponsored news that is bound to present "both sides" so as to avoid bias.[11] That kind of promotion of a certain kind of voices, especially when they are advocating the oppression of marginalized people, leads to people thinking they know *about* us without *knowing us*. We are erased from our own narratives.

Non-binary individuals, across racial lines, have been handed a set of controlling images about both our gender and our race that define who we are within the collective. AFAB white people are expected by and large to be housewives (even now) and to let white men be the "real leaders." AFAB Black people are often cast as angry or confused about their place in the world, creating a sexual politics that objectifies them both as tempting and subservient. No matter the image, the control is the important part. As Faucette notes, in quoting Melissa Harris-Perry's *Sister Citizen*, "The social world is not a positive mirror but a carnival mirror, with images of the self stretched or shrunken by a distorting surface that cannot produce an accurate image."[12] As a result, marginalized groups become accustomed to divvying themselves up, presenting polished sets of images, none of which reflects who they truly are. In an environment where the full self must be closeted, marginalized groups develop coping mechanisms that signal to their oppressors that they are at least somewhat cooperative with the overarching ideas of themselves.

This is frequently the life non-binary people live prior to coming out. We learn to play at femininity or masculinity, many of us not succeeding because it is like wearing an ill-fitting suit with a collar that's just a little too tight. Eventually, coming out as fully ourselves becomes a matter of life and death: we must be who we are outside of the gender we were assigned, or we will choke to death on the strictures of the image demanded of us. Judith Butler, who started publicly referring to themselves as non-binary in 2020, said in an interview with British pundit Owen Jones, when talking about the anti-trans lobby:

> [They don't] understand what the existential crisis is for a trans person who is burdened with a name that doesn't fit, burdened with a sex assignment that doesn't fit. If you are forced to live with that assignment, you can become suicidal. If you are forced to live with that assignment, you are effacing and denying something absolutely fundamental about who you are. It stops your ability to breathe to eat to move to live to love to inhabit the world and to call upon the world to recognize you as you are, your social and existential reality. It's not a mere feeling. It is indispensable for one's life. It's not a luxury. It is a way of living, it's a way of loving, it's a way of flourishing, and it's a way of affirming oneself in the world.[13]

Finding our language, finding the identity, even if it's "just" recognizing that we are queer, that we deviate from the norm, is vital to our sense of self-worth, for our sense of being in the world. It encompasses everything from how we see ourselves when we look in the mirror to how we move through space and time as we go about our daily lives. To deny even our interior selves access to the labels and language that help define our existence is to deny our claim to humanity.

But, as I have explored in this work, even coming out has its own issues with the controlling images of what we see as non-binary and what fits under the labels of "transgender." The center of the question for many is whether or not medical intervention is necessary and if that makes someone "trans enough" to count. This question is why I have, mainly, avoided the label of "non-binary trans." There are non-binary people who seek out medical treatment to conform their bodies to their image and who refer to themselves as "non-binary trans." I do not see myself in the "trans" label so much as I see more of myself in the "non-binary" label. So is trans then defined by medical intervention? Perhaps. But perhaps we need a larger umbrella for the entire community, not just something cobbled together from decades of changing lexicons. Many arguments for using "trans" to label the entire community, including non-binary and binary, have felt retroactive; it's "trans" because we are "transgressing" gender lines feels like a theory chosen to fit the word rather than words chosen to fit the theory.

Instead, I find myself thinking more and more about the "gender-expansive community." In the broadest sense, everyone is part of this community because no one conforms 100 percent to their assigned gender. But it also allows a great deal of room for those whose assigned sexes truly do not fit and who try on different names and labels. All the term describes is that we have an assigned sex, and our identity does not fit with whatever cultural, social, and philosophical connotations come with that label. Instead of the trans* umbrella, which has mostly become a cumbersome metaphor, perhaps we are instead all standing in the shade of a large tree, where different branches all come off the central principle of being a gender-expansive community. One of the main branches off the trunk is the binary trans community, where a person assigned one gender becomes the other at the end of the binary spectrum. Another branch shoots out from the trunk, connected in part to the binary trans but forming its own area: the non-binary community, with smaller branches for all the different labels used within that community.

We are different parts of the same tree, our roots resting in the idea that queerness is a good in itself and is not merely a separate function from heterosexuality but its own thing altogether. And within that comes connected but distinct identities each as individual as the leaves on the sequoia redwoods. Perhaps instead of dividing ourselves into the trans community and the gay community, we could recognize that we are all parts of a whole, broadly connected by the idea of "queerness."

The research supports such an idea too. David Valentine, the anthropologist who studied ballroom culture in the 1990s, discussed how members of this subculture didn't cast themselves as numerous ever-more-specific labels. They were "gay"; they were "queer." Sometimes they'd use "transsexual," but most of the time, they had their own language that developed out of their particular subculture at the intersection between poverty, queer identity, and Blackness. One of the most potent cultural examples we have of this is *Paris Is Burning*. It is from the ballroom queens that we get terms like "shade," "vogue," and "a read." And the people profiled were extremely aware that their position in society was the result not of their own choices but of the oppression of a world that boxes and labels them and throws them away because of the labels put on them.

We've never really had a chance to sit and think about labels because our community has, by and large, just been concentrating on survival. Dorian Corey says as much in *Paris Is Burning*: "I always had hopes of being a big star. But as you get older, you aim a little lower. Everybody wants to make an impression, some mark upon the world. Then you think you've made a mark on the world if you just get through it and a few people remember your name. Then you've left a mark. You don't have to bend the whole world. I think it's better to just enjoy it. Pay your dues and just enjoy it. If you shoot an arrow and it goes real high, hooray for you."

Just getting through it is enough, sometimes. And we developed our own language, our own ways of signaling to each other who we are, our own subcultures that we don't necessarily want to make known to the oppressors. Avory Faucette argues that the question should instead be reframed to ask, "What gives you the power and authority to do this [labeling]?" Should we not recognize our own position as able to label ourselves, to decide who and what we are, in a radical reclamation of our position, of no longer just getting through, but instead owning ourselves, our labels, our hopes, and our desires?

If there's one thing I want readers to understand from this work, it's that language creates and reflects meaning in reality, and for far too long, the trans and gender-expansive community has been denied access to the language we need to define ourselves. Our terms get rewritten and stolen from us. Our "femme realness queens"[14] get hijacked to describe the white gay man who does drag, not the brown trans sex worker. Our non-binary constructions get diluted by critics and oppressors who want to destroy what meaning we have found in our terms and labels. Our slogans and ideas about ourselves get decontextualized and slapped onto political campaigns, constantly neutered and tempered to appeal to the widest possible audience. We are the creators of a culture that has been stolen from us time and again, robbing us of our terms.

So now, it's time to own what we are, who we are, and claim our language for our own. We are the genderfucks, the genderqueer, the agender, the non-binary, the majesties of challenging and understanding that gender is a mere suggestion, not a death sentence. Dr. Grace Lavery, a transgender professor of English at the University of California at Berkeley, wrote in *Foreign Policy*, "The fact of trans people

cannot itself be a matter for debate, despite the eliminationist fever dreams of Raymond's inheritors in the British
High Court. Vital and profound questions about sex, gender, nature, and nurture do not end when one accepts the
fact of trans life—those questions are profoundly enriched
by our presence in the world."[15] Our presence, our existence
in the world, is of great benefit to the discussion of who we
are as a people, of what a truly feminist community looks
like, and we must be allowed to name ourselves within that
context.

So develop your own names, your own language, to
describe what you are. We're all branches off the same tree,
individual leaves waving in the wind, each one of us unique
and individual but still connected to and drawing support
from the whole. We are the gender-expansive community,
the trans community, the non-binary community. We are
us. We are them. We are the expanse between and the gaps
and the in-between.

9

SISTERHOOD, NOT CISTERHOOD

*Real names tell you the story of things they belong to in my language,
in the Old Entish as you might say. It is a lovely language, but it takes a
very long time saying anything in it, because we do not say anything in it,
unless it is worth taking a long time to say, and to listen to.*

—Treebeard in J. R. R. Tolkien's *The Two Towers*

My best friend, Esther, decided to convert to Judaism a couple years ago. She's a deeply curious person, talking circles around me in terms of discussing philosophy, logics, and rationality, and often refuses to accept "that's how it is" as a suitable answer to any question. At times in our friendship, I found myself wishing she would turn it off for a moment, but any momentary annoyance is immediately brushed aside by her putting a concept in a way that finally makes sense to me. We spar in discussions, generally agreeing, and pushing each other to think better—in fact, it was largely thanks to ongoing conversations with her about the trans community that I recognized my own non-binary identity and developed the thought that drives large parts of this work. So her conversion to Judaism didn't come as much of a surprise.

She, like me, was raised Christian but not as hardcore evangelical as me. She was a basic midwestern Methodist who found much of Christianity incoherent, particularly evangelical salvation narratives. For her, they seemed coercive and troubling. There's an old story of a missionary arriving on an isolated island, and he tells the Indigenous people there about how all people are sinners, and therefore they need to repent. An Indigenous person looks at him quizzically and asks, "What happens to people who don't know to repent?"

"Well, if a person is ignorant of the need to repent, then I suppose they don't necessarily need to," the missionary replies.

"Why did you tell me, then?" the Indigenous person replies incredulously. "You've condemned all of us to hell!"

My best friend was the first person to point out to me that a practice that requires a person to be convinced they are inherently bad and that your religion is the only way to fix it is a cruel practice and psychologically harmful. I've long left behind the individualistic conception of sin that dominates the evangelical church, but her pointing out just how cruel the project of evangelism is made me look back at my past in horror.

After her conversion to Judaism, she talked with me about what drew her to that particular faith. For one, they don't proselytize. Indeed, Jewish people discourage converts, and converts are typically met with "You sure? You're really, really sure? No, you aren't. Really?" kind of back and forth. Not that Jewish people are disbelieving that someone would want to convert, but they know what a serious thing it is and want to ensure that a person is approaching becoming Jewish with a clear heart and with complete understanding of the task they are undertaking.

The second motivation, for her, was that they believe deeply in asking questions. She's the one who introduced me to the joke that one could have three Jews in a room and five opinions about the same topic. This encouragement of questions, of debate, and of challenging tradition while also honoring it appealed to her curious nature and desire to keep moving, keep digging. And, last, she liked that she didn't necessarily have to believe in what atheists snarkily call a "skydaddy" to engage in all the debate and discussion and maintain faith. She found a home at the synagogue, and it has become a centering point for her life.

As a former evangelical, I'm constantly unpacking things I used to believe, and now with a Jewish best friend, I find myself going through ideas I used to hold about faith and rules and religion in general and realizing just how much of the Christianity I was taught is deeply antisemitic in its core. Many Christians believe in a supersessionist theory of their faith (also known as replacement theology): that Jesus's coming supersedes Jewish teaching and makes it irrelevant. "Jesus was a Jew," they'll proclaim while also saying that he fulfilled the law and the prophets and made it so we don't have to follow all the old rules anymore. This idea, however, places Jews as an enemy of the gospel, relics of a time gone by who simply don't know any better.

I found this all out when I was talking with Esther about what evangelicalism calls "legalism." There's a concept in evangelical Christianity that people who continue to follow rules, who set up rituals for their faith, are not truly faithful and instead are relying on going through the motions to draw themselves closer to G-d. I threw the term out casually while we were out shopping one day, and she stopped dead and said, "You mean rules-following like keeping kosher and keeping Shabbat and following Torah?"

It was like a wave hit me. I realized in an instant that what I'd been trained to see as a harmless aspect of Christian theology, an internecine criticism of a certain kind of Christian, was actually a rejection of Judaism. It was, quite plainly, antisemitic. I stood there for a minute, thinking, and finally said, "I never thought about it that way. Holy shit, a lot of what I've been taught is just straight up antisemitic." My brain raced through different evangelical things I'd believed and just accepted as fact and recognizing that a lot of them were actually built on rejecting Judaism. The idea of replacement theology, the idea that Christians didn't need to "follow the old rules," the idea of individual sin versus a corporate brokenness—all of it stemmed from a direct refutation of the Jewish way of thinking and the Jewish way of life.

I was gobsmacked. In the years since, Esther has become my sounding board for whether or not a Christian belief is antisemitic. Through her, I've befriended a number of other Jewish people, and while I don't always get it right, I've been working hard to be an ally to the Jewish people, understanding, too, that they are not a monolith as a people but that I should largely trust when they say something is antisemitic, even if I don't see it that way right away. I've learned to lower my defenses, to trust that they know what they're saying and that our culture is structured such that it has become impossible to avoid symbols and ideas of antisemitism that are built deeply into our culture.

I previously wanted to make this chapter an angry polemic about refuting people who are bigoted against trans people, who argued that those of us in the community shouldn't have the right to access the bathroom that matches our gender or remain safe in gendered spaces. I even wrote up a draft about how these bigots misuse studies and have poor, inconsistent internal logic.

Then I realized: I'm never going to convince the bigots. My own humanity isn't something I should have to *make an argument for*. It's nonsense to think, likewise, that I'm going to convince anyone who is hell-bent on being anti-trans to reconsider their position, whether I approached it kindly or angrily. If they were already reading this book with a mind toward "debunking" me, I wasn't going to convince them in a chapter. No one could.

But what I can do is help you, the cisgender reader, to recognize some built-in deep-seated bigotry in our culture and work it out. Like my Jewish friends who kindly remind me of antisemitic stuff that's buried deep into our cultural history, I want to sit here with you and help you to understand my story, my life, and my community. I'm not here to give you fuel to argue back against anti-trans bigotry—that's about as useful as a Jewish person debating their own humanity with a neo-Nazi. What I am here to do is empower you to recognize bigotry and bias in yourself and learn new patterns of thinking in order to be better as people, as allies, and as cisgender persons.

First: Question Yourself

The first thing cisgender people tend to do when they encounter trans or non-binary people is try to work out how we could possibly arrive at our identities. The idea that "thinking about gender" is somehow confusing or strange is a very cis-centric way to look at the concept of gender identity. Many of us didn't just wake up one day and consciously decide that we were trans or non-binary. Quite often, we knew something was "off" but didn't have the language or concepts to explain it. I had to do so much reading before

I came out about my identity—I wanted first and foremost to be an expert on myself and what my gender meant to me. Cis people in general haven't had to do that kind of thinking. Many of them have not gone through a process of trying to find the right words and then eventually landing on "cis." "Trans," to many cis-identified people, has always been cast as the other, the abnormal, the different one.

I humbly request that cis people attempt to do the same work trans and non-binary people have done in thinking about themselves. Not just a feelings check but a real, deep inquiry. Take some time to write down what describes you, both gendered and ungendered. Then think about what you think describes a man, a woman, a non-binary person. Genuinely challenge yourself to think about where your identity fits in that realm. Ask yourself: Why do I believe I am a man? What makes me say I am a woman? Interrogate beyond the biology: Would I still feel like I am a woman if I lost my uterus? Would I still identify as a man if I got testicular cancer? What parts of myself do I see as vital to my gender? Question who you are, what made you cisgender, and attempt to put yourself, mentally, into a body that reads differently from your current one.

Before you start doing anything with trans people, you need to interrogate yourself about why you believe you're the way you are. It's like asking a gay person why they're gay; it's just as reasonable to ask a straight person why they're straight. Trans people can't be the only ones taking on the burden of introspection and thinking carefully about their own gender. Once you've done the work on yourself, you'll probably understand a bit better what it's like for transgender and non-binary people to be who they are. All of us think about our gender and have worked out arguments about who we are. You're just catching up.

Second: Respect the Labels

During the pandemic of 2020, I spent most of my time in my four-hundred-square-foot apartment. I joked early in April of 2020 that by the time this whole thing was over, I'd have redesigned my entire apartment. How little did I know at that time! By June, I'd ordered a cat scanner and set up my book library on LibraryThing, a library cataloging system for my collection of books. After several international moves and losing one or two boxes in storage, my library numbers about three hundred books, and they're organized on my shelf by genre and then by author within that genre. But doing that work also meant that I had a few books that fit into multiple categories or didn't quite fit in any of the existing categories. Patrick Radden Keefe's *Say Nothing* is a historical record of the Troubles, but it's also a true-crime mystery. So I clumsily stuck it in between John Douglas's *The Killer Across the Table* and Michelle McNamara's *I'll Be Gone in the Dark*, while Simon Winchester's *Krakatoa* sat farther down the shelf among my war nonfiction works.

Every so often, I'll study my bookshelf, look at the titles, and move around the books depending on whether or not my thinking on its genre placement is different that day. I could just look up the Library of Congress placement, which would give me a call code and a category, but knowing the system as I do as a former library worker, I also know how the decisions about cross-genre books sometimes don't make a lot of sense—somehow Foucault's three-book series on sexuality ends up next to Chris Hayes' *Twilight of the Elites*. Sometimes the labels imposed upon a thing don't make a whole lot of sense for those familiar with the thing itself—example being that my first two books frequently appear in two different parts of the bookstore, depending on who is stocking them, despite them both being broadly under the genre of women's studies. (It will be fun to see where this one ends up!)

So I'm not surprised that cis people who have never really had to deal with minority genders are confused by a seemingly infinite proliferation of gender identities and labels when it feels like there should be just a few that each person fits into. It felt like just a few years ago, this whole non-binary thing didn't exist or wasn't nearly as prominent. Surely we don't need all these options? Surely there are just a few people that can fit into them?

Not really, no. Asking someone to fit themselves into a certain specific label that's only kinda sort of right is like when a white person gives their Indian friend a nickname because "Karamavir" is just too complex for them to say all the time. It's technically a thing that person will respond to, and it maybe sort of fits, but it will always not be quite right. That's our gender labels. People will find what works to describe themselves. Understand that from the get-go, and any new label will strike you not as odd and confusing but as "oh, that's a new one I've not heard of. Can you tell me more?" That's it. That's all it takes. Basic respect that means you want to understand, not judge.

Third: Don't Make Us Manage Your Feelings

Back when I thought I was cisgender, I struggled with pronouns if someone announced a change and I'd been accustomed to using a specific one. After mixing it up for a while, I also realized that it was unhelpful for me to keep apologizing every time I did, typically because my apologies drew attention to the fact that I'd made an error. I was forcing trans people to bear my feelings about my mistakes, begging for forgiveness each time. But the reason it kept happening was because I simply wasn't taking the time to practice with myself. Mentally, I still thought of the person as their assigned gender because I hadn't mentally flipped over to their new name. And I was something of a jerk in not doing that.

We in the gender-expansive community don't need to be your feelings manager or your pronoun police. When you misgender us, we can usually tell if you were doing it deliberately or as a mistake. All we ask in that moment is for you to correct yourself and move on. Don't grovel or apologize or talk about how terrible you feel. Don't make us manage your emotions about your inability to remember our pronouns. Correct yourself, move on, and then when you are not around us, *practice*. Go home and say to yourself, "This is my friend Dianna. They use 'they/them' pronouns. They take the bus. They shop at Target, and they like dark-roast coffee." Practice saying normal sentences describing your friends with their new pronouns, and your brain will start moving them over into the new category.

Fourth: Don't Be So Serious

One of my favorite Twitter accounts nowadays is the Gender of the Day. It's a bot account that randomly tweets, "Today's gender is . . . " followed by a random collection of things. "Today's gender is a flamboyance of fearsome narwhals," reads one. "Today's gender is a shimmering caribou," reads another.[1] This delights me because it's often absurd and serves to highlight—at least for me—the nonsense that is gendered experience. It's a fun little laugh in the midst of a timeline that's usually yelling about the latest political event or disaster. And the more I've talked with and become a part of the trans community, I've realized just how deeply important humor is to our existence.

For trans and non-binary people, just living through every day is sometimes a rough prospect. We face misgendering, potential violence, and fear in going out in the world as our authentic selves. So a lot of us have learned to make jokes about our lives to lighten ourselves up and laugh. Sometimes these jokes get very dark—gallows humor is part and parcel of the trans experience. Other times, these jokes are about cisgender people and "gender reveals." Lots of times, the jokes are lampshading the concept of non-binary, pretending to be confused by our own genders (let's face it, sometimes it *is* confusing!). If we tell these jokes around you, a cis person, that usually means we feel safe enough to joke around about our identities with you and that we know you'll laugh along. Not every discussion about our gender has to be serious. Lighten up and laugh with us. It makes us feel safe, too, and lets us know that you get it.

Fifth: Ask Questions (Just Not *Those*)

When I came out as non-binary on social media in October 2020, many of my friends either congratulated me on getting to know myself better or asked a simple question: "What pronouns should we use for you?" I was elated and somewhat unprepared. I'd started using they/them professionally (this book was already in talks when I officially came out) but hadn't really prepared anything for my coming out. I honestly didn't think many people would care. But my cis friends immediately demonstrated that they wanted to make sure they respected my identity. It meant a lot that people both asked questions and weren't afraid to do so.

One benefit that the increased visibility of trans people has had on our culture is that we now have an etiquette available to us for when a friend comes out. We know—from embarrassing incidents with Katie Couric and Laverne Cox—that asking about surgeries and genitals is a no-go. We know there's no reason to ask for a person's dead name. The AP has style guides for talking about us in professional journalism, for goodness' sake. We've made it!

But sometimes cis people read this as "you can't ask any questions." Like any interpersonal relationship, that's a pretty unreasonable standard. Coming out is a big change, and it's natural to have questions. If you're close enough to a person, you can usually feel out if a question is OK. One of my friends texted me to ask what his kids should call me as I've been acting as a proto-aunt to them for years. We talked it through and decided on Entle. My sister-in-law texted me about whether or not this new identity means I'm trans. I explained to her what I've explained throughout this book—that sometimes it means "transition"; sometimes it doesn't. I don't know that I want to take testosterone. I do know I might want top surgery at some point. Does that make me trans? I don't know right now, and that's OK.

Imagine it this way: if you had a friend who announced a pregnancy, you would allow them to set the boundaries about what is and isn't appropriate to ask. Follow that same guide with your transgender and non-binary friends. You're not going to ask your friend who just gave birth how their vagina is doing unless you're *really close*. So don't ask me about mine.

Sixth: Let Us Be Vulnerable

Christmas 2015 was spent abroad. I was living in Oxford at the time, and a local friend invited me and our New Zealander friend back to his parents' house for Christmas, an invitation we delightedly accepted. He lived in a small suburb of London, a couple hours' bus ride away. Nestled in a hillside, his small village had decorations and monuments to one of its more eccentric former residents, a man who collected a menagerie of exotic animals and would ride about town in a carriage drawn by a group of zebras.

We spent Christmas Eve in a local pub, playing cribbage (which I taught them to play) and having drinks together. The pub was crowded, with groups of people home for the holidays and out for a drink to escape home for a little bit and catch up with old friends. One particular set of people was causing a commotion in the pub—even for me, as the loud American in the group, this group's loudness was distracting. Two English women were at the center of the noise, and they were visibly drunk. One of them fell in the middle of the pub, laughing, and the other tried and failed to help her up. We tried our British best to ignore them.

Later in the evening, my pint of Coca-Cola hit me, and I went to use the facilities. At the time, I looked much like I do now, just thinner. I sported short hair with part of it shaved in what's commonly called an undercut. I wore a sweater and jeans. I pushed open the door to the women's room only to be greeted by a sight that's since been burned into my mind. One of the drunk women was sitting on the toilet, pants around her ankles, with the stall door wide open. Several friends were surrounding her, as though she were in labor. The woman on the toilet saw me, took in my short hair and boyish outfit, and started *screaming*.

I couldn't tell everything she said through the noise, but I caught "Get out of here!" I ducked into the other stall to the noise of her friends trying to assure her, "That's a *lady*!"

I was visibly shaken up when I got back to the table. I was genuinely afraid—while I hadn't yet begun identifying as non-binary, I'd gotten a taste here of what it's like when someone perceives you correctly and hates what you are. My friends, who are heterosexual and cisgender, comforted me as best they could and understood that my evening had been completely altered by that one instance. They affirmed that the drunk lady was in the wrong, that this was not the norm, and that I was safe with them. Having my friends be understanding of my pain and allowing me to express my fear without minimizing or dismissing it was deeply important in that moment. Being friends with trans and gender-nonconforming people means understanding that they have different fears and anxieties and sometimes read situations as threatening where you may have trouble spotting the threat. Listen and trust that when your friends say they are not safe, they are not safe, and you have a duty of care to help them in whatever way is most needed.

—

This is, of course, not a definitive list, because the queer community is not a monolith. It is a general guide for how to be better people around us. My last bit of advice would be to make sure we don't have to always fight our own battles. I have had friends tag me in when they're dealing with a particularly persistent string of harassment or trolling over their identity, and I will hop in and draw fire away from them. This can be done in person or online. It takes a lot for us to simply survive through the day, and having someone who is willing to stand by our side and either help us fight our own battles or fight them for us is a big boon to getting through the day.

A story went around Twitter once from a guy who was sitting at a new bar in a neighborhood he'd just moved to. He was chatting with the bartender, when another patron came in and sat down. The bartender took one look and pointed to the door: "You. Get out. Now." The guy got up and left without so much as asking for a drink.

"Why'd you do that?" the original patron asked. "Did he do something?"

The bartender motioned to his chest and said, "He had some Nazi symbols on his jacket, and with them, you gotta cut it off quick. If you're nice and serve him, he'll come back around next week and start becoming a regular. Pretty soon he starts bringing his Nazi friends with him. And by then, it's too late. You're now the Nazi bar, and you can't kick them out because they're shitty, and after all, you've been serving them this whole time, so why stop now that it's a bigger group? You gotta head that whole thing off at the pass."[2]

The thing about being an ally or just being a good person is that it's easy to do when the person in question is right there. It's easy to remember, "Oh, this person is X" when you're staring them in the face and they can implement consequences right then and there. What's harder is ensuring that you are remaining consistently allied even if that person is not there. Bigots tend to know enough not to show their bigotry toward the marginalized people in question—at least, most of the time. They have a sense of wanting to avoid public embarrassment or shame that can help keep their bigotry in check, at least around others.

But when bigots get in groups where they think everyone around them shares their own identities, they will become more open. They will test the waters with a sly joke to see if you pick up on the more abhorrent views suggested. They will sidle into the bar wearing a jacket with a flag of Rhodesia on it. They'll venture to say a slur or an anti-trans comment to gauge your reaction. If you don't react or if you react positively, you're in. You're now friends with a bigot. Congratulations, you suck.

Shut that shit down, even if it's hard. Even if it's "just the way that friend is." You have to let people know that their bigotry won't be tolerated around you. Give them social consequences for their actions. Stand up for us when we're not in the room. This is what it takes to commit to your queer friends.

—

Back in 2016, I called my dad the night before the election. My mom, his wife of forty-two years, had passed just two years before, and I'd thrown myself into doing work I thought would make her proud. Despite being raised as a Republican, when I turned eighteen, I registered as an independent, and by my midtwenties was voting for progressives and Democrats up and down the ticket. Dad and I never really saw eye to eye politically, but my brother and I thought Trump would at least be a dividing line. In 2016, Trump was still largely unknown, and Democrat fears over his fascist tendencies—calling for the jailing of his opponent, veiled racism surrounding claims of voter fraud— were at that time largely cast as overblown. With an open spot on the Supreme Court, my dad knew Trump would put in a pro-life candidate, and that ultimately convinced him to cast his vote for Trump in an early vote the Sunday before the election. He told me he regretted it instantly.

Four years later, the stakes of the election that could result in another four years of Trump were stark. Hundreds of thousands had died from a pandemic his administration badly mishandled with little federal response that could've been used for supplies. The national deficit soared, and democratic norms had crumbled. We thought, for sure, Dad couldn't possibly be considering voting for Trump a second time. When I told him I would probably need a break from time with him if he did indeed vote for Trump a second time, he handwaved away my concerns, calling them mere political disagreement. But I pressed further, telling him about how Trump had rolled back protections for people in my queer community, that I could be left for dead because a paramedic has a "personal belief" about queer people.[3] I asked him, "Doesn't that matter to you, that these policies could be used to put me and my community in danger?"

When he hesitated, my world fell apart. He heard the catch in my voice as I asked him, "Dad, what do *you* believe about gay people?" He deflected, saying that he'd always treated me with kindness and that he'd been perfectly friendly with my previous girlfriend. "But do you think I'm going to hell?" I asked, knowing the answer was one I wasn't going to like.

"I'm not sure" came his halting response down the line. In that moment, I knew I could never be as close to my father as I had been. He had been hiding how he felt about me, covering it with kindness, believing that if he just showed me he loved me enough, it would make up for the fact that he was mourning the straight, cisgender daughter he wanted me to be. He would never show up to Pride with me. He would have "problems" attending a wedding, should I ever get married.

When I got off the phone, I called my brother, crying. I told him what Dad had said and that we wouldn't be talking for however long it took. My brother said OK, said he loves me, and that I am absolutely OK just the way I am. And most importantly, he said he would do his best to work on Dad on my behalf. My brother is a chaplain with an MDiv from a well-respected seminary and went through his own journey of coming around to accept LGBT people. He made himself a safe person to cry to about what was happening with our father because he had taken the steps to affirm and understand me as I am, as a queer person, as a non-binary person, as his friend and sibling. *And* he promised to put in the work to make our family a safer place for me too.

This is what the stakes are. Your choices can make the world better for our community, or complacency can make it worse. We aren't going anywhere, but sometimes we're just tired of having to be our own advocates all the time. You must stand in for us when we cannot stand for ourselves, hold the line when we are failing, and be willing to take on just a small bit of the risk we take in living our authentic selves every day. Love only wins if we fight for it.

10

WHO TELLS YOUR STORY?

*If people bring so much courage to this world, the world has
to kill them to break them, so of course it kills them. The world breaks
everyone, and afterward, many are strong at the broken places.*

—Ernest Hemingway, *A Farewell to Arms*

By all rights, I shouldn't know Kitty Genovese's name. I shouldn't have encountered her in high school in a story about the importance of action when a stranger is in trouble. Her story should've ended the way many of us hope ours will, with her life coming to a close surrounded by loved ones, quietly, peacefully, in her old age. But that was never to be for Kitty.

Kitty Genovese was just twenty-eight years old when a man decided to follow her home from her parked car in the early morning hours of March 13, 1964. Kitty was coming home from her work as a bartender, headed back to her apartment in Kew Gardens in New York City. Winston Moseley, a Black man from Manhattan, was in the habit of sneaking out of the house he shared with his wife and children and cruising the streets of New York City looking for women to attack. That night, his target was Kitty Genovese.[1]

Kitty parked her car just one hundred feet from her apartment building's front door and began the walk back, when Moseley stepped out from the darkness and began pursuit, eventually catching up to Genovese and stabbing her twice in the back. She screamed, alerting neighbors, one of whom yelled for the man to leave her alone. Moseley left the scene, only to return a few minutes later as an injured Genovese lay in the building's vestibule, having lost the strength to unlock the interior door and pull it open. Moseley proceeded to stab Genovese several more times before finally raping her and stealing nearly fifty dollars (approximately four hundred dollars in 2021). A neighbor found her shortly after Moseley left and cradled her in her arms until the police arrived.

A few weeks later, the *New York Times* would publish an untrue but unforgettable story about how the brutal attack took place in view of thirty-eight people and not one of them did anything.[2] The sensationalist article gave rise to a psychological concept called "the bystander effect," where people in crowds who witness something happening will assume that someone else will take care of it. The death of Kitty Genovese became a cautionary tale not only for people who may be witness to tragedy but also to victims of it. As a child, I was taught to scream "fire" instead of "help" to encourage bystanders to act more readily; people will respond to a house on fire, but they may not respond to someone calling for help, not wanting to get involved in trouble.

Years later, I learned much more about Kitty than the simple *New York Times* retelling of her death gave us. She was a bartender who held down two jobs to save up money to eventually open her own Italian restaurant. She was a lesbian. Her "roommate" at the time was actually her girlfriend, and they'd been together for a year. She was a badass who had built an entire life for herself, and she was a happy and proud member of the queer community, which, in 1964, was not always the easiest thing to be.

What's more, though, is that the more research was revealed about the attack that ended her life, the more complicated and complex everything became. Not only was Kitty gay, but several of her neighbors were. One of them, who peeked out his door to see Moseley attacking Kitty in the hallway, was a gay man who hesitated to call the police not out of callousness but because the police were a major antagonist of the queer community at that time—they frequently raided gay clubs and arrested gay people for the crime of being gay.[3] It's understandable that a gay man would be afraid to call the cops directly, so he called friends and told them what was happening, and those friends called the police.

Queerness complicates narratives. Simple stories of a white woman not receiving help from cold, callous neighbors is actually instead a story of a community afraid of police brutality, frozen by fear, and hampered by a lack of city infrastructure (911 would not be introduced for several more years). It took research and interviews and investigation to turn up the real story, one of oppression, mismanagement, and an ongoing battle between a marginalized group and the power of the state. Historians have worked hard to reclaim the narrative of a woman whose identity was erased because of homophobia and police brutality in an age when gay people were demonized and dehumanized. Kitty did not get to live to tell her story, but the work in reclaiming who she was as a lesbian, as a woman, as a human full of ideas, hopes, and dreams is ours to do. As we've learned throughout this book, it is important that we keep our own stories, our own histories, alive, if only so that others in our community may know that they are not alone.

We don't always have control over the narratives people tell about us, especially if we are silenced by death, violence, or discrimination. This is why I am insistent on contextualizing and understanding stories as they were for people in that time. It is the stories we hear, the lives of those from before and those strangers we may never meet but with whom we have something in common, that shape our world and our politics. This was the reasoning behind the movement in the 1970s for gay people to come out of the closet, to reclaim our narratives and our stories, to refuse to allow the bigots to tell our stories for us.

After all, it was the story of one trans person that got me started on my own gender journey, largely because I saw the clear injustices happening. I saw how quickly one injustice compounded upon another and found myself identifying with Cece's plight—and then, eventually, with her identity as a trans woman. McDonald's position was uniquely changed by her race and socioeconomic position in society, and as something of a baby feminist at the time, I saw how the varying loci of oppressions merged to become one unique oppression, falling upon the Black trans body with immense force.

I learned of Cece McDonald shortly after her arrest in 2012. McDonald is a Black trans woman who was outside a restaurant in Minneapolis's east side, around the Cedar-Riverside area, when a group of mostly white people began harassing her and her friends with racist and transphobic comments. One of the people in the harassing group hit McDonald in the face with a bottle of alcohol, slicing open her cheek.

As the groups began fighting, McDonald fled, only to be followed by one of the men from the group—a man who allegedly said she looked like a "dude tucking his dick in."[4] McDonald took a pair of scissors from her purse and stabbed the man in the chest. He died that night, and McDonald was arrested and charged with second-degree intentional murder. It was later revealed that the victim had a criminal history and, in an autopsy photo, was revealed to have a swastika tattoo. McDonald maintained that she acted in self-defense following racist and transphobic comments, in addition to being physically attacked by the man's ex-girlfriend.

The state first offered a plea of first-degree manslaughter, which McDonald refused because she believed she had been defending herself. But as the pretrial proceedings wore on, McDonald eventually accepted a plea for second-degree manslaughter—a charge carrying a sentence of forty-one months, as opposed to the forty years to life from the murder she was charged with. Doing so meant giving up her claims to self-defense and admitting guilt.[5]

But adding insult to injury, McDonald was then sent to serve out her sentence in a men's prison. She was initially denied access to her hormone treatments, though pressure and publicity eventually restored her rights to receive the proper medical care. But because there was no precedent in Minnesota for transgender inmates being housed in accordance with their gender identity, McDonald had to endure a year and a half in two different men's prisons, an assignment that the state said was in accordance with their assessment of her gender.[6]

Not only had this young woman survived an attack from a man who approached her with violent racism and transphobia and whose friends assaulted her, but she then spent her time in prison sharing a space with cisgender men—a vulnerable woman placed in a dangerous situation. Following her release in 2014, she used her publicity to talk about life in prison as being unsafe for anyone, much less transgender people. She now uses her platform and advocacy to highlight the cruelties of the American prison system, arguing that *no one* is safe in prisons and that we need alternatives that allow for reform, rehabilitation, and reconciliation. McDonald put herself back into the narrative and refused to be cowed by the state.

For centuries, this is what gender-expansive people have been doing. We have always been part of the narrative— and now we are nearly as visible as we were one hundred years ago when Magnus Hirschfeld traveled America telling stories of our lives and loves. A world war and a culture war later, we are still working on telling those stories, both of the past and of who we are now. These stories are so often inflicted by and covered in the blood of our ancestors in the movement—those taken from us by the sacking of the Institut für Sexualwissenschaft, those taken by bigotry and violence. But it is also so full of life—the life of Dr. Alan Hart, who worked to find therapies for tuberculosis patients and developed lifesaving medications; the work and ministry of the Public Universal Friend, who elevated the marginalized and cared for those whom white supremacy would destroy; and the lives of countless queer people who, for centuries, have toiled in quiet anonymity, simply doing what needed to be done to make the world a better place.

At the end of *Paris Is Burning*, Carmen Xtravaganza talks about how getting gender-affirming surgery and her legal documents in order made her feel like she was finally the person she was meant to be all along: "I feel great. I am very happy. And I feel like the part of my life that was a secret is now closed. I can close the closet door, there are no more skeletons in there, and I'm as free as the wind that is blowing out on this beach."[7] There is sheer joy on her face as she holds her hands up as if to embrace the sun shining down on her. She dances a little, taken up in the joy of realizing who she is outwardly finally reflects who she has always wanted to be. This is her moment, her story, her joy.

Her life didn't magically get easier. She remained in the ballroom scene in New York, a representative of the House of Xtravaganza for another three decades. She works the modeling scene, is famous in her own circles, and is proudly, fully, who she is. I know about her now because of the hard work of documentarians and historians who have worked to make queer history clear and accessible for future generations. And she is freer because she was allowed the room to change her narrative, to become who she knew herself to be, to embody her true self.

I've always loved wearing button-down shirts, especially as I embraced my butch identity when I was still thinking of myself as a gay woman. But button-downs didn't always love me. I had to size up to make sure my boob gap was covered, often making my thinner arms look wonky with sleeves that extended down and covered the top of my hands. The first time I put on a binder, I grabbed one of the button-ups I'd brought home earlier that year, only to discover the dreaded boob gap made it impossible to wear. As I buttoned it up, staring down at my body with wonder, I saw the boob gap disappear, the buttons lying flat and the shirt resting comfortably, not pulling or stretching in uncomfortable ways.

I almost cried. I quickly snapped a picture and sent it to a friend, captioned, "OMG MY BINDER MAKES MY SHIRTS FIT!!!!!!!" I finally had the look I wanted. I finally felt like I read the way I wanted to be read. It was what I'd seen others refer to as gender euphoria. Looking down at my body gave me joy, not consternation, for once in my life. And I felt myself clawing back my own narrative, presenting to the world who and how I wanted to be, no longer hiding behind sweaters and baggy T-shirts. This, too, is the gender experience: the joy you feel when you finally look down at yourself and see who you've wanted to be this whole time.

Each of us, queer or not, is living a life that is a complex, complicated narrative that cannot be summed up in simple ways. When I was a teenager, I had a conversation with my uncle who is a pastor about how I wanted to go to college for theology and I felt G-d was calling me to learn more about G-d's church and to embrace ministry. I was a goody two-shoes white lady from the Midwest with mostly A grades who always came home on time and was never invited to parties. My uncle considered for a minute and then joked, "You know what you gotta do? Go off and get addicted to heroin, then get clean and come back. Then you'll *really* have a story." We both laughed knowingly: we'd both heard the testimonies, the compelling narratives of someone fallen deep into addiction who was saved by the call of Jesus. We also knew implicitly that the stories that sell both in evangelical ministry and in wider culture were neat arcs of redemption, of the person lost and confused and finally saved by something. In evangelical culture, it was finding Jesus in a hotel-room Bible while on a week-long bender. In popular culture, it was finally getting clean when you had a kid or when you met that one person you could love. The power of change in these stories is almost always something outside of the self: another person, a relationship, or a religion. But so rarely are narratives so neat and tidy, and sometimes the saving mechanism is simply our own understanding of who we are coming into being.

Whether this book confirmed for you who you are or made you think about who you possibly could be, I want you to keep moving forward into the future with the confidence that even if you don't yet know, you are on your way. No one can determine for you who you are. It is yours to determine, yours to decide, and yours to become.

Our stories are ours to own. It is we, as a gender-expansive queer community, who have relied constantly on each other, creating new chosen families when our biological ones have rejected us, creating new selves to present to a world that finds our queerness confusing and threatening. We are embracing everything that has been put upon us and turning our pain into joy. Our cultural memory is imbued with all parts of the queer experience so that we remember both how hard this struggle has been and that the struggle was all completely worth it, to arrive at who we need to be.

Coming out is a vital part of that project. Visible queerness challenges the norms and assumptions society has built around us. I urge you, if you are in a situation where it is safe to do so, to close that closet door behind you, to step out into the sunlight.

I had the pleasure of going on a business trip to San Francisco a few years ago. I'd never been before, but as a queer person, I was excited to visit a place with so much queer history embedded in it. I found a free afternoon at the conference and took the train over to the Castro, a traditionally

queer neighborhood that was the home base of city supervisor Harvey Milk, the first openly gay person to hold
elected office in the country. Milk's story, memorialized in
a biopic back in 2009 by writer Dustin Lance Black, was a
life of joy and sorrow forever intermingled. In fighting back
against Anita Bryant, an antigay activist from Florida, Milk
urged people in California to come out so that people could
see and understand that queer people weren't some Other,
some shadow lurking in the corner, but instead they are
your neighbor, your child, your parent, your cousin, your
brother. Because so many brave people stood up and spoke
out, my nieces will grow up in a world where being who
they are will not necessarily be tinged with terror and fear
but rather marked by great joy and community. Because
of my open presence in their lives, they will always have a
person to point to who has made being genderqueer, non-
binary, *whatever* a normal thing.

During his short tenure as a member of the board of
supervisors before his tragic assassination at the hands
of a fellow city supervisor, Milk made speeches and public comments that made it clear that he knew where he
sat as a representative of the gay community, of the queer
community. In 1978, he stood on the steps of city hall and
spoke about how important this visibility is: "Invisible, we
remain in limbo. A myth. . . . And the young gay people
who are coming out and hearing Anita Bryant on the television and her story. The only thing they have to look forward to is hope. You have to give them hope. Hope for a
better world. Hope for a better tomorrow. Hope for a better place to come to if the pressures at home are too great.
Hope that all will be alright."[8]

There is hope to be had, if only we work to see it and
give it and be it. I might be the first non-binary person

you have encountered. But I will not, most assuredly, be the last. Or you, in your queerness, in your coming out, in your being, are part of a great community that stretches back generations and will stretch forward in time, going on and on, each generation renewing hope that our fore-bears did not struggle in vain, that being who we are is worth something in this wild and wonderful world. Our hope sits in the complicated, complex stories of who we are, as queer people, as parents, siblings, family, friends, strangers, lovers. When we remember who we are, we have hope.

ACKNOWLEDGMENTS

This book couldn't have made it to this point without the encouragement of Hannah Bowman, my agent, and Lisa Kloskin, my editor. Even as they were working with an experience distinctly outside of their own, they treated all of it with great respect and made my work better.

To Max and to Dani: conversations with you helped this work come to fruition. Your friendship has been indispensable both in helping me figure out who I am and in making sure my ideas come across. I cannot possibly thank you enough for your understanding when I texted late at night with an idea, for your willingness to read early drafts, and for your challenging questions as I worked out what message I wanted to send.

To the trivia team—Emmy, Michelle, Austen, Ari, Anna, and Ryan (and little A!): here's to nights at the brewery and winning based on knowledge of obscure theory and biblical languages.

To my Sioux Falls Happiness Crew: thanks for understanding me as I've grown to understand myself more. Here's to many happy getaways and no feeding of the squirrels.

To my brother and sister-in-law, Marc and Carrie, and the niblings: you made coming out an easy AF process, and I'm so glad to have family who loves and embraces all of who I am.

To the Minneapolis Central Library and the Walker Branch: I am sorry for printing a hundred pages in one go. I was not even sneaky about it. I owe you $20.

NOTES

Introduction

1. Sandy Stone, "The Empire Strikes Back: A Posttranssexual Manifesto." ACTLab, UT Austin, 1987.

Chapter 1

1. Simone de Beauvoir, *The Second Sex*, trans. Constance Borde and Sheila Malovany-Chevallier (London: Vintage Books, 2009), 293.
2. It should be noted that Weil's rejection of her own Jewish history led her to a rejection of Judaism and what she saw as Judaism's influence on the world, despite the fact that her own theories closely mirror Jewish mysticism. Weil's rejection of the Jewish should rightly be read as antisemitic and therefore should be held in tension with her conceptions of "self" as described here.
3. Simone Weil, *Gravity and Grace* (New York: Routledge & Kegan Paul, 1952).
4. Butler identifies as nonbinary and uses "they/them" pronouns for the large part.
5. Ludwig Wittgenstein, *Philosophical Investigations*, trans. G. E. M. Anscombe, P. M. S. Hacker, and J. Schulte (Boston: Blackwells, 2001), 54.
6. Wittgenstein, *Philosophical Investigations*, 77.
7. Jacques Derrida, *Of Grammatology*, trans. Gayatri Chakravorty Spivak (Baltimore: Johns Hopkins, 2016).
8. Jean Baudrillard, *Simulacra and Simulation*, trans. Sheila Faria Glaser (Ann Arbor: University of Michigan Press, 1994).
9. The *Matrix* analogy, by the way, is no accident—the Wachowski siblings, both of whom came out as transgender years after the film—had all the key stars read Baudrillard's *Simulacra and Simulation* during filming.
10. Judith Butler, *Gender Trouble* (New York: Routledge Classics, 1990), 201.
11. Butler, *Gender Trouble*, 198.
12. Butler, *Gender Trouble*, 187–88.

13. Susan Stryker, "My Words to Victor Frankenstein above the Village of Chamouix," *GLQ* 1, no. 3 (1994): 252.
14. Stryker, "My Words to Victor Frankenstein," 253.
15. Stryker, "My Words to Victor Frankenstein," 246.
16. Stryker, "My Words to Victor Frankenstein," 253.
17. Stryker, "My Words to Victor Frankenstein," 254.
18. Owen Jones, "Owen Jones Meets . . . Judith Butler," *Owen Jones Meets*, YouTube, January 1, 2021.

Chapter 2

1. T. G. Wilfong, "Gender and Sexuality," in *The Egyptian World*, ed. Toby Wilkinson (New York: Routledge, 2013), 211.
2. A note: I use Common Era for dates here.
3. Samantha Schmidt, "A Genderless Prophet Drew Hundreds of Followers Long before the Age of Non-binary Pronouns," *Washington Post*, January 5, 2020.
4. For example, ongoing arguments about whether or not businesses that serve the public can refuse service to same-sex couples or transgender individuals on the spurious basis of "religious conviction."
5. Schmidt, "A Genderless Prophet."
6. Schmidt, "A Genderless Prophet."
7. Austen Hartke, *Transforming* (Louisville, KY: Westminister John Knox, 2018), 51.
8. For those coming from an evangelical context, Rashi holds the same status in the Jewish world as Ellicot's or the Pulpit's Commentary do in evangelicalism. He is studied in depth and is one of the primary commentaries consulted when studying Torah.
9. Hartke, *Transforming*, 61.
10. Abigail Shrier, *Irreversible Damage* (New York: Regnery, 2020).
11. Indeed, with a newly calibrated search on JSTOR with "gender identity disorder" + "teenagers," I found articles going back to 1996 that mention teenage female to male transsexuals in discussing their psychology.
12. J. K. Rowling, "J.K. Rowling Writes about Her Reasons for Speaking Out on Sex and Gender Issues," J. K. Rowling Official Website, June 10, 2020.
13. Susan Stryker, *Transgender History* (Berkeley: Seal Press, 2008), 33.
14. Stryker, *Transgender History*, 34.

15. Hanne Blank, *Straight: The Surprisingly Short History of Heterosexuality* (Boston: Beacon Press, 2012), 3.
16. Blank, *Straight*, 55.
17. Blank, *Straight*, 57.
18. Lewis Cope, "Sex Change Operation Can Mean 'Life or Death' to Patient," *Minneapolis Star Tribune*, December 18, 1966, 1.
19. Janice Raymond, "Facts and Fictions about Transsexual Empire," Janice Raymond Official Website, n.d.
20. C. Riley Snorton, *Black on Both Sides* (Minneapolis: University of Minnesota Press, 2017), 177.
21. Snorton, *Black on Both Sides*, 179.

Chapter 3

1. Hugh Ryan, "What Is Trans* and Where Did It Come From?" *Slate Magazine*, January 10, 2014.
2. Susan Stryker, "Transgender Studies: Queer Theory's Evil Twin," *GLQ* 10, no. 3 (2004): 214.
3. Stryker, *Transgender History*, 33.
4. Chris Hayes, "Why Is This Happening: Protecting Trans Rights With Chase Strangio," *Why Is This Happening*, NBC News, September 23, 2019.
5. Judith Butler, quoted in Ki Namaste, "Tragic Misreadings: Queer Theory's Erasure of Transgender Subjectivity," in *Queer Studies: A Lesbian, Gay, Bisexual, and Transgender Anthology*, ed. Genny Beemyn (New York: NYU Press, 1996), 188.
6. Judith Butler, quoted in Ki Namaste, "Tragic Misreadings," 188–189.
7. David Valentine, "The Categories Themselves," *GLQ* 10, no. 2 (2004): 216.
8. Valentine, "The Categories Themselves," 218
9. Valentine, "The Categories Themselves," 219.
10. Kate Bornstein, "My Gender? Oh, It's Nothing," *New York Times*, June 19, 2019.
11. David Valentine, *Imagining Transgender: An Ethnography of a Category* (Raleigh, NC: Duke University Press, 2007), 31.
12. Valentine, *Imagining Transgender*, 24.
13. Valentine, *Imagining Transgender*, 34.
14. Valentine, *Imagining Transgender*, 38.

15. Valentine, *Imagining Transgender*, 39.
16. Jason Robert Ballard, "Identifying as Truscum Is a Disservice to Yourself," *FTM Magazine*, n.d.
17. Jack Halberstam, "On Pronouns," Official Website, 2012.
18. Judith Halberstam, "Transgender Butch: Butch/FTM Border Wars and the Masculine Continuum," *GLQ* 4, no. 2 (1998): 289.
19. Halberstam, "Transgender Butch," 303.
20. Petra L. Doan, "To Count or Not to Count: Queering Measurement and the Transgender Community," *Women's Studies Quarterly* 44, no. 3 and 4 (Fall/Winter 2016): 98.
21. Halberstam, "Transgender Butch," 306.

Chapter 4

1. @sullydish (Andrew Sullivan), "What does it *feel* like to be "non-binary"? If it means not a stereotype of men or women, join humanity. If it means neither male nor female, and nothing to do with either, you're a different species altogether," Twitter, December 1, 2020, 7:32 PM.
2. Stryker, *Transgender History*, 33.
3. George Chauncey Jr., "From Sexual Inversion to Homosexuality: Medicine and the Changing Conceptualization of Female Deviance," *Salmagundi* 58/59 (1982–1983): 117.
4. Chauncey, "From Sexual Inversion to Homosexuality," 121.
5. Stryker, *Transgender History*, 35.
6. Blank, *Straight*, 58.
7. Chauncey, "From Sexual Inversion to Homosexuality," 122.
8. Chauncey, "From Sexual Inversion to Homosexuality," 123.
9. Chauncey, "From Sexual Inversion to Homosexuality," 124.
10. Karin A. Martin, "Gender and Sexuality: Medical Opinion on Homosexuality: 1900–1950," *Gender and Society* 7, no. 2 (June 1993): 250.
11. Chauncey, "From Sexual Inversion to Homosexuality," 128.
12. Note: this is the term used in the research at the time; today it would properly be called "intersex."
13. Michel Foucault, *The History of Sexuality*, vol. 1: An Introduction, trans. Robert Hurley (New York: Vintage Books, 1990), 42.
14. Hilton Dresden, "Today in Gay History: France Becomes First Western European Country to Decriminalize Sodomy." Out. com, October 6, 2016, https://www.out.com/today-gay-history/

2016/10/06/today-gay-history-france-becomes-first-west
-european-country.

15. Susan Stryker, "Responses to Psychoanalytic Practices
     Encountering Queer Theories," *Clinical Encounters in Sexuality*,
     ed. Noreen Giffney and Eve Watson (Goleta, CA: Punctum
     Books, 2017), 423.
16. Stryker, "Responses to Psychoanalytic Practices," 425.
17. Jones, "Owen Jones Meets . . . Judith Butler."

Chapter 5

1. Abigail Shrier, *Irreversible Damage* (Washington, DC: Regnery
    Publishing, 2020).
2. Also herein known as binary trans.
3. Jay Prosser, "No Place Like Home," *Modern Fiction Studies* 41,
    no. 3–4 (1995): 504.
4. Reminder: Halberstam is a trans man who still accepts "she/her"
    when referring to work published under his dead name.
5. Halberstam, "Transgender Butch," 303.
6. Shrier, *Irreversible Damage*.
7. Shrier, *Irreversible Damage*.
8. We talk more with KC in chapter 7.

Chapter 6

1. Da'Shaun L. Harrison, "Affirming Trans People Means Caring
    for AMAB-Non-binary Folks Too," DaShaunHarrison.com.,
    January 13, 2021.
2. Petra L. Doan, "To Count or Not to Count: Queering
    Measurement and the Transgender Community," *Women's
    Studies Quarterly* 44, no. 3 and 4 (Fall/Winter 2016): 105.
3. Doan, "To Count or Not to Count," 101.
4. Adrian Silbernagel, "Gender Euphoria: The Bright Side of Trans
    Experience," *Queer Kentucky*, October 14, 2019.
5. Erin Paterson, "Where Are All the Happy Queer and Non-
    Binary Stories?" *British Vogue*, January 30, 2021.
6. Erin Paterson, "In Lockdown, I Have Finally Felt the Glorious
    Possibilities of Gender Euphoria," *British Vogue*, November 21,
    2020.
7. Flan Park, personal interview, February 23, 2021.

8. Paterson, "Where Are All the Happy Queer."
9. Helena Darwin, "Doing Gender beyond the Binary," *Symbolic Interaction* 40, no. 3 (1997): 326.
10. Darwin, "Doing Gender beyond the Binary," 326.
11. Sandy Stone, "The Empire Strikes Back: A Posttranssexual Manifesto." ACTLab, UT Austin, 1987.
12. Bornstein, "My Gender? Oh, It's Nothing."

Chapter 7

1. Aubrey Gordon, *What We Don't Talk about When We Talk about Fat* (Boston: Beacon Press, 2020), 98–99.
2. Francis Ray White, "Fat/Trans: Queering the Activist Body," *Fat Studies* 3, no. 2 (2014): 90.
3. There's disagreement about whether or not to hyphenate 'non-binary' as a term. I have chosen to use the hyphen because it linguistically emphasizes that we are separated out from an alleged binary, and different from it.
4. "Two-Spirit," Indian Health Services. Online.
5. Sarah Viren, "The Native Scholar Who Wasn't," *New York Times*, May 25, 2021. Online.
6. CBC Radio, "What Being Two-Spirit Means to Indigenous Elder Ma-Nee Chacaby," CBC Radio Online, June 19, 2017.
7. Gordon, *What We Don't Talk about When We Talk about Fat*, 72.
8. Max Malament, personal interview, January 26, 2021.
9. K. C. Slack, personal interview, February 17, 2021.
10. Francis Ray White, "Embodying the Fat/Trans Intersection," in *Thickening Fat: Fat Bodies, Intersectionality, and Social Justice*, ed. M. Friedman, C. Rice, and J. Rinaldi (London: Routledge, 2019), n.p.
11. Francis Ray White, personal interview, February 2, 2021.
12. White, personal interview.

Chapter 8

1. "So What Is Non-Binary?" Mumsnet.com. Online.
2. Avory Faucette, "Fucking the Binary for Social Change," in *Counterpoints: The Gay Agenda*, ed. Gerald Walton (New York: Peter Lang, 2014), 74.
3. Faucette, "Fucking the Binary for Social Change," 75–76.

4. Patricia Hill Collins, *Black Feminist Thought* (New York: Routledge, 2008), 69.
5. Collins, *Black Feminist Thought*, 69.
6. Collins, *Black Feminist Thought*, 71.
7. Collins, *Black Feminist Thought*, 71.
8. Jennie Livingston, Paris Is Burning (Off-White Productions, 1990).
9. Bell V. Tavistock, Case CO/60/2020, Royal Courts of Justice, Judiciary, UK, P 24, https://www.judiciary.uk/wp-content/uploads/2021/09/Bell-v-Tavistock-judgment-170921.pdf (p. 24).
10. "Analysis: Gillick Competence Wins the Day in Puberty Blockers Appeal," *Irish Legal News*, September 24, 2021, https://www.irishlegal.com/articles/analysis-gillick-competence-wins-the-day-in-puberty-blockers-appeal.
11. Katherine O'Donnell, "The High Court's Ruling to Limit Access to Puberty Delaying Medication for Trans Teens Was the Latest Blow in What Feels to Many Trans Brits Like an Endless Onslaught of Prejudice," *Daily Beast*, December 10, 2020.
12. Faucette, "Fucking the Binary for Social Change," 78.
13. Owen Jones, "Owen Jones Meets . . . Judith Butler," *Owen Jones Meets*, Youtube, January 1, 2021.
14. Livingston, Paris Is Burning.
15. Grace Lavery, "A High Court Decision in Britain Puts Trans People Everywhere at Risk," *Foreign Policy*, December 15, 2020.

Chapter 9

1. @Genderoftheday (Gender of the Day) on Twitter.
2. @IAmRageSparkle, "I was at a shitty crustpunk bar once getting an after-work beer. One of those shitholes where the bartenders clearly hate you. So the bartender and I were ignoring one another when someone sits next to me and he immediately says, 'no. get out.'" Twitter, July 8, 2020, 10:48 AM.
3. This Trump-era policy was rolled back early in the Biden administration, reinstating protections for LGBTQ+ people who were first instituted with the passage of the Affordable Care Act in 2010.

Chapter 10

1. Robert D. McFadden, "Winston Moseley, Who Killed Kitty Genovese, Dies in Prison at 81," *New York Times*, April 4, 2016.

2. Nicholas Goldberg, "Column: The Urban Legend of Kitty Genovese and the 38 Witnesses Who Ignored Her Blood-Curdling Screams," *LA Times*, September 10, 2020.

3. Gillian Brockell, "'Wrong, Plain and Simple': 50 Years after the Stonewall Raid, New York City's Police Commissioner Apologizes," *Washington Post*, June 6, 2019.

4. Nicole Pasulka, "The Case of CeCe McDonald: Murder—Or Self-Defense against a Hate Crime?" *Mother Jones*, May 22, 2012.

5. Pasulka, "The Case of CeCe McDonald."

6. Paul Walsh, "'CeCe' McDonald Freed after 19 Months in Prison for Killing Mpls. Bar Patron," Star Tribune, January 13, 2014.

7. Livingston, Paris Is Burning.

8. Harvey Milk, "The Hope Speech," June 25, 1978.